the value of housing design and layout

a research project commissioned by CABE and ODPM in association with Design for Homes

produced by FPDSavills Research with Davis Langdon & Everest

CABE, the Commission for Architecture and the Built Environment, is the nation's champion for better places, places which

- work better
- feel better
- are better

We believe that decent homes, work places, shops, schools and hospitals are everyone's basic right, a right worth fighting for. CABE uses its skills and resources to campaign for a better quality of life for people and communities across England. We do this through a rich mix of campaigning, researching, instigating and assisting with technical expertise and opinion.

CABE
Tower Building
11 York Street
London SE1 7NX
Telephone 020 7960 2400
www.cabe.org.uk

ODPM
Eland House
Bressenden Place
London SW1E 5DU
www.odpm.gov.uk

Design for Homes
79 Parkway
London NW1 7PP
www.designforhomes.org

Copies of this report are available on CABE's website at www.cabe.org.uk
or from:

Thomas Telford

The Customer Services Department
Thomas Telford Limited, Units I/K
Paddock Wood Distribution Centre
Paddock Wood, Tonbridge
Kent TN12 6UU
Tel: 020 7665 2464
Fax: 020 7665 2245

www.thomastelford.com

ISBN 07277 3208 0

Design by Kneath Associates
Printed in Great Britain by Latimer Trend

Foreword

Sir Stuart Lipton
Chairman
CABE

England will need at least another three million homes by 2016. Yet last year an estimated 160,000 were built, far short of the Government's target of 225,000.

National opinion surveys consistently show that a significant section of the house buying public would never consider purchasing a new house, preferring more established neighbourhoods and building stock.

We have to accept that to date we have not provided a product that enough people are willing to buy into. Where demand so grossly outstrips supply, there is little commercial incentive for housebuilders to offer more innovative and attractive designs. So consumers are left without a choice.

But we need to take account of the fact that people see value in good design and that this will attract them to modern housing. Innovative thinking, integration with existing communities and investment in quality are the things which will persuade people that they want to live in modern housing.

Well designed housing improves quality of life for residents and the wider community, helps reduce crime, fosters community cohesion and significantly reduces whole life costs.

This CABE/ODPM commissioned report seeks to demonstrate a way of measuring the economic dividends of investing in high quality housing design and layout. It provides a methodology that developers, funders, planners and housebuilders can use for comparing different housing sites and schemes.

It is especially timely given pressure from the Government who rightly insist that new housing development, especially in the south-east of England, should be aiming for densities of over 30 units per hectare.

We do not want to repeat recent mistakes – soulless estates, cramped housing and inefficient neighbourhood layouts. We want to see houses where people aspire to live and stay. Investing in the design of these new buildings and, just as importantly, in the quality of the public space between them is imperative if we are to deliver the neighbourhoods of tomorrow.

Sir Stuart Lipton
Chairman
CABE

Contents

Executive Summary

Executive summary

This report attempts to assess the extent to which design changes the value of residential development. It sets out a methodology whereby different types of design in housing and housing layout are examined to see how their differences affect the commercial value of new developments for developers.

This research pilots a methodology that can be used to compare housing on any site in any location. Developers, funders, planners and other interested parties will be able to use this methodology on any site to make a like-for-like comparison between different developments.

The methodology and the results from the small sample are intended to act as a framework for further, ongoing investigation into the role of good design in housing (or what is deemed to be good design) and its effects on value.

The focus of this study is to demonstrate what, if any, enhanced value there is for the developer in building well designed schemes, broadly upholding the urban design principles in PPG3, compared to building more recent standard examples of housing layout and design. It is not concerned with whether the capital values of individual properties may or may not be higher than a comparably sized, standard new home. Neither does it examine the amount of capital appreciation that individual homes within the more innovative schemes may enjoy compared to more standard properties.

The research selected eight examples of completed developments and compared them in four matched pairs. It was intended that four schemes with certain 'innovative' design elements would be compared against four of a more 'standard' design in the same location. Practical difficulties in obtaining confidential commercial information from certain developers necessitated creating two hypothetical comparator schemes sharing the same locations as two of the schemes with innovative design elements. The remaining two matched pairs both comprised real schemes. The eight sites were studied in four different locations around the South East. This had the effect of eliminating the impact of regional economies and the differences between regional housing markets when making comparisons.

The developments were costed and a market valuation made. A residual value was then calculated on each scheme and expressed on a per hectare of land basis (using the same overall measure of land for each example) so that all sites could be compared to each other on a like-for-like basis. The residual value *does not* represent land value; it represents the commercial value to the developer of the site.

With such a small sample and the pilot nature of this project, the headline results were inevitably inconclusive, inasmuch as they neither proved that innovative design and layout improves developer value nor did they disprove it. A number of themes emerge which, while not necessarily statistically significant, are of importance, especially as a basis for further research validation.

Of the four locations studied, three of the four 'exemplar' (innovative design) schemes yielded higher residual values than the 'conventional' schemes (standard design) and one yielded poorer residual values to the developer.

The widespread market perception that good design costs more was borne out by the study, but not completely. All of the exemplar schemes cost more to build per square foot of gross internal area than the standard comparators.

The notion that higher density decreases value per square foot was not supported by this study. In two of the four cases, the value of the units in the higher density scheme was greater on a per square foot basis than the comparable lower-density schemes (in one case, substantially so).

Only in one scheme (Surbiton) was there a clear and definitively enhanced added value in the "exemplar" scheme where residual value was enhanced by more than 15% over and above the standard scheme. In the case of two other exemplar schemes (Bishop's Stortford and Chelmsford), values appeared to be enhanced by the nature of their design (by 7.5% and 10.3% respectively).

Residual value per area of land

Scheme	Location	Residual value per: Hectare	*Acre*	Difference to matched pair in same location
A	Surbiton – exemplar	£12.4m	*£5.0m*	+15.3%
B	Surbiton – conventional	£10.7m	*£4.3m*	–13.3%
C	Bishop's Stortford – exemplar	£4.6m	*£1.9m*	+7.5%
D	Bishop's Stortford – conventional	£4.3m	*£1.7m*	–6.9%
E	Chelmsford – exemplar	£3.8m	*£1.6m*	+10.3%
F	Chelmsford – conventional	£3.5m	*£1.4m*	–9.3%
G	Aylesbury – exemplar	£3.5m	*£1.4m*	–4.7%
H	Aylesbury – conventional	£3.7m	*£1.5m*	+5.0%

Source: FPDSavills

There appears to be no clear-cut relationship between how big a site is and whether innovative, PPG3-led design is more profitable or not based on this small sample. However, the clearest example of added development value was found on the largest scheme. This may be because a large scheme has the greatest opportunity to create its own sense of place, while smaller schemes are more vulnerable to the influence of externalities and even other developments on adjacent sites.

Sites with relatively high residual values, in relation to their matched pairs, appeared to have high proportions of public open space in relation to the overall size of the site.

In addition to establishing the methodology, one of the most important aspects of the research is the identification of some possible trends in managing higher density, better designed schemes to maximise net development value. There is a critical balance to be struck by the developer in maintaining unit values while increasing density. In the schemes studied, some developers have achieved this while others have not. Striking this balance is possibly the single most important issue in determining the commercial value of PPG3-compliant schemes for the developer. This alone is reason enough to advocate design practices that achieve increased value environments, while at the same time increasing density. In these situations, the increased value achieved is far in excess of the extra build cost incurred.

The study also raised the question of the extent to which the design and layout of a large development scheme can affect local externalities, that is how it can actually change the nature of a place and how it is perceived. One developer's innovative designs on one part of a larger development area could be a positive influence on the value of more conventionally designed housing on another part of a site.

This research begins to illuminate the question: 'what makes a desirable location?' Estate agents emphasise 'location' as the most important element of housing value. Leaving aside macroeconomics, there is a series of factors, including the built form, which creates a sense of place. Some of the developers in this study have helped to show that it is possible to create a sense of place, and therefore a new type of location on a piece of land, by employing certain design principles. These new places may be more desirable, and therefore more valuable, than their neighbours. They may also be more desirable and valuable than they would otherwise have been had standard development house types and layouts been employed. Further research using the methodology developed in this study is urged to confirm this.

When it comes to value for a developer, as opposed to an owner-occupier, it may be more appropriate to talk about 'density', rather than 'location'. The issues involved are complex but the rules of the game now seem to be to maximise unit values while increasing the number of units on the site to meet planners' requirements. This is not a new game, but changing planning rules have increased the stakes. Whereas before a developer might have aimed for densities of between 25 and 30 per hectare (10 and 12 per acre), new planning and design technologies have raised the target to 30 to 40 per hectare (12 to 16 per acre) in suburban locations. In urban situations, these densities would be very much higher again.

There is a strong argument that values will only be maintained at these densities if design techniques become very much more sophisticated to maintain their attractiveness to occupiers.

This study begins to show that good design becomes more and more critical as densities are increased over and above PPG3's benchmark of 30 units per hectare. Standard design and standard layouts will not work on high-density developments. Increases in density must accompany increased attention to design quality: there are clear commercial rewards when this course is followed.

Introduction

1.0

1.0 Introduction

The Commission for Architecture and the Built Environment (CABE), with support from the Office of the Deputy Prime Minister (ODPM) and Design for Homes, commissioned a research study to:

1. create a methodology which could determine the relationship between housing value and perceived housing quality and
2. show how this impacts on the developer

FPDSavills Research addressed these questions primarily in relation to betterment to the developer. The report shows the impact of the value of different types of design to developers by examining the influence that design has on the residual value, left after all site development and marketing costs have been taken into account. This residual sum potentially impacts on developer margins. It provides an approach to answering the question of whether different types of design in housing and housing layout affect the commercial value of new developments for a developer.

The research programme has been both experimental and practical. It provides a methodology that can be used on any site in any location or situation to compare sites of different types in other locations. Developers, funders, planners and other interested parties will be able to use this approach on any site to make a like-for-like comparison between different developments.

This report is designed to ask the question and give an indication of whether what is deemed to be good housing design adds value to property or not. As such, it is intended to act as a framework for further, ongoing investigation.

1.1 Context

The issue of good design in housing has come to the fore recently in a variety of ways. The Urban Task Force report *Towards an Urban Renaissance*, in 1999, advocated the improved design quality of the urban fabric in regeneration schemes large and small. The document concentrated on design principles in the context of planning and policy rather than in the context of the commercial world and development businesses.

In 2000, the DETR followed hot on the heels of the Urban Task Force report with the, now familiar, *Planning Policy Guidance Note 3: Housing*, commonly referred to as PPG3. This document broke new ground in requiring higher density new development and setting out some of the design principles to ensure its higher quality. Underlying this move is a shift in the planning paradigm that new developments should be about building places rather than just predicting need and providing the basic accommodation to fulfil that need. It was significant in introducing detailed design principles into the planning system.

Other initiatives and movements have brought the issue of urban design, housing design and layout to the forefront of development, architecture and planning. Arguably, in other countries design issues have been more widely accepted and were taken on board earlier by mainstream, commercial developers. In the USA, for example, the New Urbanist movement has rapidly gained acceptance and credibility. The design, community, sustainability and urban form principles have been adopted and endorsed in the commercial real estate world on that side of the Atlantic for some years now. August bodies such as the Urban Land Institute publicise and promulgate such principles. In the UK, it could be argued that these principles have been taken up on a smaller scale and have not yet found such widespread acceptance in the commercial world of housing development. While the Urban Villages Forum, CABE and other bodies have subscribed to some, but not all, of the New Urbanist design principles, these principles have been taken up by relatively few developers. Many of the developers who have employed new design principles have tended to be in the social housing or non-commercial sector, rather than mainstream housebuilders.

New Urbanism is not synonymous with the best practice, innovative design now advocated by CABE and other interested British bodies. Specifically, planned communities do not really fit the UK context, nor does the insistence on traditional architecture. The reference here to New Urbanism is made to highlight the contrast with the US experience, where commercial organisations have adopted new and different design methods on a wider scale than has hitherto been the case in the UK.

However, the situation is changing. During the period of this research project, the authors have noted a shift in the number of development schemes where developers have adopted at least some of the design principles of higher density, mixed tenure, contemporary architecture and layout. An increasing number of schemes appear to have adopted higher densities, mixed tenure and permeable, walkable road layouts and connections.

Much of this shift is largely attributable to the increasing adoption of PPG3 at the local planning level, forcing developers to build designs and layouts that, in most cases, they would not otherwise have considered. One area where this new approach is particularly noticeable is in Essex where the authors found widespread conformity to the progressive *Essex Design Guide* in many new developments. Another county where the authors noted a widespread adoption of new design principles was in Dorset, home of the now famous New Urbanist village scheme of Poundbury.

The increase in PPG3-compliant schemes around the country means that it is becoming difficult in certain areas to find the more familiar, homogenous housing estates that most people associate with modern housebuilding. It was noticeable that in areas where 'best practice schemes' are to be found, planning requirements have created a spate of similar examples and a corresponding reduction in the development of lower density, 'feeder road and cul-de-sac' type layouts. However, this was found to be a localised phenomenon. Across the country as a whole, the authors could still identify a plethora of housing development schemes built as single tenure, similar sized, standard housing types, arranged in cul-de-sacs, off feeder roads adjacent to bypasses on the edge of town, built at densities of less than 25 units per hectare.

It appears likely that the trend towards the more sophisticated design principles of innovative high density has been led by some, but by no means all, local planning department requirements rather than developers themselves, at least initially. Having said this, it would appear that some developers have seen a commercial advantage in developing sites according to at least some of the PPG3 principles. Discussions with developers revealed that some increasingly believe that they can enhance property values and, more importantly, their margins by designing and building in these new ways. Other developers remain to be convinced.

It is exactly the proposition that certain types of design can add value that we set out to test in this study. In order to do this, we have devised a method by which the value of a development scheme to the developer can be measured. We are not interested in how the capital values of individual properties may or may not be higher than a comparably sized, standard new home. Neither are we concerned with the amount of capital appreciation that individual homes may enjoy compared to more standard comparisons. The concern of this study is to demonstrate what, if any, enhanced value there is for the developer in building schemes following the urban design principles of PPG3 compared to building more standard examples of housing layout and design.

Addressing the gaps

2.0

2.0 Addressing the gaps

2.1 Introduction

A review of the existing literature highlights a number of significant gaps, not least a lack of empirical evidence examining the commercial value to the developer of investing in high quality housing design in urban locations. Throughout the 1990s, a developing body of literature highlighted a growing awareness of the issue of the quality of urban design in the built environment, and residential design began to attract academic attention. The publication of the report of the Urban Task Force, *Towards an Urban Renaissance* (1999), gave a major policy impetus to issues of urban design, including the design of residential development. The Urban Task Force argued that, 'the challenge of reducing construction costs and increasing quality in housing is central to achieving an urban renaissance'. However, beyond the issue of promoting good design to encourage higher residential densities and more sustainable forms of development, the report did not examine the issue of good design as a component of enhanced development value.

In a review of literature and case studies of commercial workspace by Bartlett in 2001, a key finding was that,

> ***'the research suggested that good urban design adds value by increasing the economic viability of development and by delivering social and environmental benefits'.*** *The value of urban design, 2001*

It also stated that the existence of these benefits was increasingly acknowledged across stakeholder groups. It was noted that good urban design can confer two distinct forms of benefit: direct economic benefits to those investing in development, and indirect social and environmental benefits to others and to society at large. The researchers note that the relationship between design and value is unlikely to be a straightforward correlation between better design and increased value, since the issue of cost has to be taken into account. Noting the different perspectives of the public and private sectors towards development, the research suggests that for good urban design to be valued by all stakeholders, it needs to offer distinct dividends in the short as well as the long term. The additional 'value' added by good urban design beyond that relating to the development scheme itself is now widely acknowledged.

In arriving at any assessment of the costs and benefits of improved urban design, it is evident, therefore, that the institutional context in which development takes place is critical for an understanding of the relative perspectives of the different actors and agencies involved in particular development sectors.

2.2 Housebuilding and design: institutional context

The institutional context plays a significant role in identifying the conditions under which the most profitable approach for housebuilders is to adopt standard designs.

However, the external effects created by good design are not sufficiently well researched, evaluated or understood by key players.

A pioneering attempt to undertake an analysis of private sector attitudes to design and the value of it was made by Ball in 1983 in a study entitled *Housing policy and economic power: the political economy of owner-occupation*. It indicated that, in relation to the private housebuilding industry,

> ***'design is an important component of the development process because, if used appropriately, it can enhance the revenue from a site considerably'.*** *Housing policy and economic power*, 1983

Ball argues that marketability and cost minimisation tend to pull in different directions in relation to housing design for the speculative housebuilder — although individuality in design and non-estate site layouts may improve marketability, it tends to raise construction costs and may lower site densities with corresponding increases in land costs. Housebuilders minimise this potential conflict through particular design solutions: a limited use of standard house types, with individuality achieved by cosmetic variation of the external elevations.

Ball also notes that the market preference for detached dwellings results in a design form which imposes cost considerations in excess of other design forms (by some 10–15%), but that this is more than offset by higher selling prices. He also indicates that there is no acceptable definition of housing quality in the private sector, 'so while design has become increasingly linked with the growing market orientation of speculative builders, associated with this trend has been a continuing fall in new housing standards'. Ball argues that this is not primarily due to the pressure of rising land costs, but derives from the precise institutional structure in which private housing production in the UK takes place.

Subsequent research has confirmed that the use of standard house types has become prevalent among large and medium-sized housebuilding companies, and that this is driven by the institutional context and the pressures of market competition associated with private sector housebuilding. Moreover, it has been concluded by Hooper and Nicol that,

> ***'what is most striking about the overall residential design process in speculative housebuilding is the divorce, in design terms, between house design and the design of housing layouts'.*** *Environment and Planning B*, 2000

Ball argues that the layout of an estate and the mix of houses implied by it are a key aspect of private housing development, with design a central component of marketability rather than an aesthetic adjunct to it. Others have confirmed this finding.

Ball's research highlighted the fact that the competition between landowners and housebuilders for the development gain following the grant of planning permission had focused attention on the operation of the planning system in the post-war period. A more recent attempt by Verhage and Needham in 1997 to specify the particular institutional configuration which applies in the case of speculative housebuilding in the UK, also highlighted the role of competition. It looked at the competition between the various actors in the development process to capture development gain and also looked at the mediating role of the land use planning system in this process.

Verhage and Needham state that the design outcome of a development will be dependent on a negotiation process, in which institutional arrangements regulate the supply side of the market (i.e. housing land supply). In a similar fashion to Ball, the authors note that, in this negotiating process, the possible gains on housing construction do not play as important a role as the possible gains on land development.

They argue that the land development process itself is a major influence on the physical characteristics of residential areas. In cases where a private developer is responsible for land development, it is a private agency that receives the development gains, possibly sharing them with the landowner. If the costs of secondary services are charged to the private developer by means of planning gain agreements or other developer contributions, the remaining development gains are reduced. In the case of private developers securing development gain, they say that the main objective will be to maximise profit subject to realising continuity. The authors observe, 'the developer might try to achieve this through the quality of the residential environment. If the products — the houses and their residential environment — are of good quality, the developer can set its prices higher'. The limit to this increase will be the point at which the extra expenditure equals the increase in income resulting from the higher prices.

Verhage and Needham argue (as does Ball) that the British planning system imposes an 'extra price' on housing, leading to high development gains for private developers. In the absence of a betterment tax or levy, development obligations have been structured to oblige private developers to spend part of the development gain on the residential environment, and developers view these not as fixed, but negotiable, costs.

Verhage and Needham follow through with conclusions on the implication of their analysis. They say that, if development obligations impose additional costs, this could lead to a decrease in production. Local authorities are therefore faced with a dilemma in that promoting a larger supply of housing could result in a lower quality of residential environment. Similarly, promoting a higher quality residential environment could result in a reduced supply of housing.

Leopold and Bishop, in their 1983 report *Design philosophy and practice in*

speculative housebuilding, examined the consequences of this institutional context for the process of housing design. They argued that the speculative element in land development gain in private sector housebuilding requires a type of housing which minimises the special high risks associated with this form of housing provision.

The existence of a portfolio of such designs enables developers to make a reasonable estimate of costs of production at short notice, and to make a rapid estimate of the potential 'yield' of any site. The authors observe that, 'not surprisingly, housing design, in this context, plays an inherently conservative role, one that inhibits any radical approach to housebuilding that might operate through the design process'. Booth, among others, has noted this conservatism in design to be a long-term feature of the housebuilding industry. Moreover, Leopold and Bishop assert that, 'the combination of standardised, fairly stable individual house plans with very flexible, market-sensitive elevations and trim is the physical expression of the compromise between the long-term stability of the production process and the more volatile demands of the market'.

The most recent review of housing design quality, *Housing design quality: through policy, guidance and review* by Carmona, supports these general conclusions. It argues that, 'without some public sector intervention, the unique market circumstances in which housebuilding occurs will continue to ensure the widely accepted (even among many housebuilders) devaluing of design in the residential sector'. Despite this, some commentators have noted that planning intervention in the form of design guidance may have a positive impact, creating a product with enhanced sales values and achieving development at higher densities.

In some instances, the increased certainty afforded by coherent residential design guidance is argued to be of potential assistance to housebuilders. However, it is also noted by Carmona that pressure from landowners for a share of development gain results in a situation in which

> ***'expectations are conceived in a design vacuum, with — usually — no consideration given to the cost of delivering higher quality development'.*** **Housing design quality, 2001**

As a consequence of this pressure, housebuilders often have to strategically ignore local authority design aspirations in order to make their bid. In order to avoid this, some commentators have argued that the only means of increasing residential design quality is to access the development value for investment in design.

2.3 Brownfield land development and housing

The literature on design and housebuilding is limited in that, either explicitly or implicitly, it reflects a predominantly greenfield context for housing development. As the scope for such development has become constrained by major Government policy initiatives (most notably PPG3), and particularly the sequential approach to urban land release, the potential of previously developed land for housing has received increased attention.

Research into the costs of residential development on greenfield sites appears not to have been undertaken for brownfield development. A study by Conran Roche and Davis Langdon & Everest in 1989 broke down residential development costs but did not deal explicitly with design issues.

Literature on brownfield development land by authors such as Syms presents the argument that the development of brownfield sites may be characterised by high levels of financial uncertainty. This is particularly evident in the context of the loss of English Partnership's 'gap-funding' regime. Financial uncertainty is exacerbated in the context of previously developed sites that are affected by land contamination which requires remediation. Such uncertainty may significantly affect the context of negotiation between housebuilding companies and local planning authorities, in which improved design may be only one issue among many competing, material planning considerations. In a review of progress relating to the identification of brownfield housing land, research by the Civic Trust in 1999 found a poor fit between the original identification of sites for housing and the actual achievement of successful housing development on them. Again, there was no specific reference to design issues in this research (although adverse market conditions and the unwillingness of landowners to sell feature prominently in it).

Successive studies by Llewelyn-Davies have investigated the possibilities of increasing the housing capacity of urban land. A major conclusion has been that, 'there is potential to significantly increase residential densities and at the same time improve the environmental quality of new residential development. This can be achieved through a creative design-led approach which responds to the particular characteristics of a site, its surroundings and the needs of future residents'. The essence of this approach is that the objective of quality is addressed through design rather than by applying general planning standards.

The authors state that an important consequence of this recommendation is that,

> ***'developers must invest more in design to achieve high quality development at higher densities. This means less reliance on standard types and a greater freedom for designers to respond to the potential of individual sites'.*** **Llewelyn Davies, 2000**

No explicit economic analysis of the costs and benefits of such an approach was undertaken.

Others, such as Rudlin and Falk, offer a different perspective. They advocate both urban renaissance and improved housing design. Writing in 1999, they say that, 'in both the private and social housing fields there are powerful forces at play which reinforce both suburban designs and suburban locations as well as exerting a corrosive effect on quality and resisting innovation'. They go on to indicate that, 'while there are signs that things may be changing, these forces must currently be seen as a major constraint on the promotion of more urban housing'.

A cautionary note is sounded in other research regarding the operation of the land and housing market under conditions of supply constraint in the UK. Cheshire and Sheppard in 1997 indicated that, under conditions of sustained housing demand and land supply constraints, it is generally 'planning amenities' or space that increase disproportionately in price in comparison with 'reproducible' attributes of housing. These 'goods' which the planning system delivers are valued, the authors argue, but in ignorance of the price that is paid for those planning amenities. 'Their values are not just incorporated in the price paid for a house. There are also extra costs. These are the higher price paid for all housing land, shortage of space and the more cramped conditions in which we all have to live. Planning amenities are not paid for directly so they appear to be free. But because they are only produced by restricting the supply of building land, they cause the price of land, and thus of housing, to rise.'

This analysis would seem to confirm and extend that of Verhage and Needham in identifying the source of the 'extra price' attributable to the 'residential environment' outside the dwelling unit in the operation of a restrictive planning system. Design is not, however, one of the explicit housing attributes considered in the analysis (although access to schools and to public open space is modelled). Others also make a similar argument concerning such 'neighbourhood externality' effects of planning-induced improvements in the quality of residential development.

2.4 Housing design quality and 'value'

The publication in 1973 of *A design guide for residential areas* by Essex County Council introduced a radically new framework for residential design guidance. Subsequent research into the impact of such design guidance for private residential development by the DOE/HRF in 1976 indicated a concern with the cost implications of design guidance and control. It asserted that, 'a requirement for a more expensive design solution for the houses must be offset by a saving in cost elsewhere, such as in road construction, or by allowing a higher density of development to reduce the land costs for each dwelling'.

In a discussion paper on good design in housing by Davison in 1990, it is argued that many aspects of good design add little or no extra costs to residential schemes, but that some elements of good design do increase costs. It is argued that, 'developers who have persisted with high design standards have found that their product does have an added, premium value, but only on the subsequent resale when the environment is more settled and established. This benefits discerning purchasers but does not recoup the developer's costs'.

Davison estimates that the cost of achieving a broad spectrum of design improvements might be in the order of 5–10% of the land value. He argues, 'this seems to suggest that there should be some scope for planning intervention to redirect some of the betterment from the landowners' profits to the benefit of the local community with better design, materials and open space'. It is, nevertheless, claimed that intervention of this type, using planning agreements, is difficult to achieve, except on sites not already allocated in a local plan.

In a review of the role of housing standards in promoting housing quality in 1992, Karn argued that 'not only are there no financial inducements to provide high standard new housing, there are no national targets for housing quality'. He added that, 'certainly there is now a groundswell of unease about trends in standards and quality of design'. Subsequent research by Karn and Sheridan in 1994 indicated the very different parameters that influence housing standards and design quality in the private and housing association sectors. They indicated that, 'to improve quality of design in the private sector, we, therefore, conclude that the best mechanism is to strengthen consumer pressure'.

The Government discussion document *Quality in town and country* in 1994 argued in its preface that,

> ***'Quality pays. Good quality is good economics'.***
>
> *Quality in town and country*, 1994

However, no argument or research was cited to demonstrate this assertion. In 1998, a DETR report examining ways to improve the quality of new housing layouts argued that many of the obstacles to enhancing quality are symptoms of land valuation that ignores the cost of quality and the lack of cooperation in the design process. The report argued, 'bad design can increase land values. Over-development with uniform house types laid out on minimum plots, in schemes that ignore site characteristics and local identity, will maximise the land value. Good design does not necessarily increase costs, but it is rarely able to match the land value achieved by bad design. It is therefore essential that quality targets are established before land values become fixed'.

The report also noted the role of standard house types in maximising the development value, and therefore the land value, which is considered an essential aspect of layout design in a competitive market. The limitations of these standard house types on urban redevelopment sites are recognised and the perspective of the developer is regarded as crucial. 'Developers look within the site to assess the value of the land and the commercial viability of their investment. The importance of this aspect of development cannot be overstated; it is largely through the investment of development companies that plans are realised. But commercial considerations, which should run in parallel with quality and sustainability objectives, are allowed to dominate the developer's thinking, often to the exclusion of other matters. The developer's appraisal of the setting of the site is concerned with the housing market rather than design opportunities for the development. Developers must be encouraged to take a broader view of their activities'.

Research into the external appearance and site layout of new houses, commissioned by the Popular Housing Forum in 1998 indicated that, for owners of new-build housing, 'issues of site layout were considered more important than the appearance of an individual property, especially the area in which a house was built. The appearance of the neighbourhood was seen as more important than the appearance of the individual house'.

Carmona argued, in 1999, that the issue of the dominance of roads in the determination of housing layouts is arguably the most difficult component of the residential landscape to integrate successfully. Not surprisingly, then, the current period of residential design guidance was ushered in with the publication by the DETR in 1998 of the report *Places, streets & movement, a companion guide to Design Bulletin 32 — Residential roads and footpaths*. In the same year, the publication of *Planning and development briefs: a guide to better practice* endorsed the need to consider design issues at the earliest stage of the planning and development process (a point which was made strongly in the 1998 POS/HBF/DETR report).

The publication by the DETR of *Planning Policy Guidance Note 3: Housing* in 2000 consolidated the transformation in national planning policy guidance relating to design which Carmona dates from the original guidance issued in 1992. The publication of *By design — urban design in the planning system: towards better practice* by DETR/CABE in 2000 began the process of providing national guidance relating to urban design objectives and aspects of development form. English Partnerships and The Housing Corporation published the *Urban design compendium* by Llewelyn-Davies in 2000 as a complement to *By design* to contribute to the improvement of the quality of housing-led regeneration projects and the promotion of sustainable new development. A companion guide to PPG3, *By design: better places to live*, published by DTLR/CABE in 2001 sought to apply the principles of good quality urban design (set out in *Places, streets and movement* and *By design*) to the residential environment. None of these official publications considers in detail the issue of costs and added value from improved design quality in residential environments.

2.5 Summary

The most striking finding in a review of the literature relating to the quality of residential design is the almost complete absence of any empirical attempts to measure the implications of high quality on costs, prices or values.

Few commentators have gone beyond making a distinction between the direct benefits for built environment stakeholders and those indirect benefits that accrue in the form of 'public goods' or externality effects. Initial attempts to formulate models of the residential development process which emphasise the institutional and negotiating context in which residential design solutions are formulated have tended to be based in a greenfield development context, with few applications in brownfield contexts. To the extent that brownfield developments involve complex pricing effects deriving from public goods and externality effects deriving, in part at least, from the operation of the land use planning system, the attribution of relative costs and benefits deriving from design *per se* have been difficult to isolate and measure. In particular, it becomes difficult to isolate 'value' attributes of residential design deriving from the dwelling from those deriving from its locational context.

Those who have focused on the process of residential design (at least in the private sector) have emphasised the crucial importance of the institutional framework in determining the parameters within which different actors and agencies carry out housing development. In this process, the establishment and apportionment of 'added value' deriving from design is seen to be partially contingent on the place in the development process at which crucial decisions on design are made (which are, in turn, reflected in residual land values). The apportionment of that part of the 'added value' deriving from design in the development process is dependent on the complex operation of housing and land markets, so that part of this 'added value' may appear upstream or downstream of the residential development process itself.

Very little research has addressed the issue of the commercial value of housing design to the developer. Most literature relating to architecture, planning, housing and economics only touches on the issue of the development value that results from design in the most marginal fashion. Not surprisingly, therefore, methodological discussions are virtually non-existent. Where they do occur, they usually relate to greenfield development. In the very considerable literature dealing with urban design in general, and residential design in particular, there is very little reference at all even to cost implications, let alone 'value'.

The references cited in this literature review are contained in Appendix 1.

Methodology

3.0

3.0 Methodology

3.1 Overview

The aim of this study was to define how different types of housing layout and design may affect the costs of development and the value of the end-product and, hence, how developer profitability might be affected. The following questions were addressed:

- What constitutes good design?
- How can economic value be determined?
- How can externalities be dealt with?

The research programme comprised three parts.

1. Investigate the background to the project, conduct necessary literature reviews and justify the chosen empirical methodology involving the selection and comparison of the matched examples
2. Select appropriate examples of completed developments in matched pairs to compare developments with certain innovative design elements to those of standard design. Put a cost and a market value on the developments to determine whether there is any difference in a standard measure of residual value and therefore potential developer margins
3. Examine the findings on the selected projects and discuss what forces and factors may be behind the results. Compare these to other research findings, if appropriate, and recommend any further research work that might be needed

In overview, a method was devised to compare developments on a like-for-like basis to facilitate the comparison of different schemes. This was done by comparing a series of eight examples of different types of housing in four suburban locations within the South-East. Of these developments, four (one in each location) could be described as largely PPG3-compliant, in that they employ some degree of innovative design, and were selected by the commissioners of the report to represent best practice examples (these have been termed 'exemplar' in the report). The remainder were good developments but following a more standard design (these have been termed 'conventional' in the report). Two of the 'conventional' developments in this study are hypothetical as no cooperative developers on a real development could be found to act as comparators to the exemplar schemes.

The issue of determining commercial value was done on the basis of a residual (i.e. the sum left after deducting all onsite development, construction and marketing costs from the house sales revenue). It must be emphasised here that, despite being expressed as a residual sum per area of land, this residual *does not* represent land value. The residual covers land costs, corporate overheads and developer margin. It also, importantly, represents the sum available to the developer to carry out any section 106 or other agreements to build community facilities and any affordable housing element of the development, for example. While the cost of these agreements is often critical in determining developer margin, we have not measured them. This is because they are negotiated on a site-by-site basis and

therefore vary greatly from scheme to scheme. Their inclusion in cost measurement would not therefore facilitate a like-for-like comparison to be made between schemes. The residual sum measured in this research is intended to represent both the commercial value to the developer of the site and also some of the social value since, without it, the developer could not afford to provide any loss-making social amenity buildings.

It must be noted here that, given the way the development market works, some of the residual value measured in this report would be shared with the landowner. Exactly how much depends not only on what proportion of the residual sum is used to provide social housing and other section 106 buildings and works, what is needed in the form of central company overheads, but also on the developer's negotiating position. This will be determined by factors such as the degree of competition for the site from other developers and the form of contract that the developer enters into with the landowner. No attempt was made to assess how much of the residual would end up in the pockets of the landowner rather than the developer.

The methodology was designed to compare each site on a like-for-like basis so all valuations were made at a single point in time (March 2002) and as if all units were being sold on the same (exemplar) site in each location. The measurement of land area was also standardised.

A simple, step-by-step guide to the methodology used is contained in Appendix 4. Further details of this methodology are given below.

3.2 Selection of case studies

This research used case studies of real development schemes wherever possible to avoid being unduly theoretical. The case studies in this research were selected on the basis that they represented a range of design and layout principles. Four different locations were selected, all of which contained examples of schemes that followed the urban design principles in PPG3 or innovative housing developments.

Although initially a variety of locations across the country was identified for study, it was decided that it would be difficult to identify any differences in value that were due to regional externalities and regional market differences rather than the issue of design. It was therefore decided that all locations should be in the South-East to eliminate any differences attributable to variations in regional house markets and regional economic considerations.

The sites selected were all on the edge of towns or district centres and all the sites were suburban in nature. They were Surbiton in outer south-west London, Bishop's Stortford in East Hertfordshire, Chelmsford in Essex and Aylesbury in Buckinghamshire.

All of the development schemes selected were examples of mainstream, mass house building of a good build standard. In each location, two schemes with different types of design and layout were selected. One was selected on the basis that it was largely PPG3-compliant and an example of good design practice. (Subsequently, on careful measurement, some of these schemes turned out not to be PPG3-compliant on the strict measure of minimum density.) The best practice sites were termed the 'exemplar' site in each case. The other site in each location was selected on the basis that it was a typical example of a standard design and layout type in that location. These sites were termed the 'conventional' site in each case.

The following criteria, established in *By design*, the DTLR/CABE companion guide to PPG1, were used to select the exemplary schemes.

- **Character** — a place with its own identity
- **Continuity and enclosure** — a place where private and public spaces are easily distinguished
- **Quality of the public realm** — a place with attractive and successful outdoor areas
- **Ease of movement** — a place that is easy to get to and move through
- **Legibility** — a place that has a clear image and is easy to understand
- **Adaptability** — a place that can change easily
- **Diversity** — a place with variety and choice

Schemes that broadly conformed to these characteristics were selected as the 'exemplar' schemes.

The conventional schemes were selected on the basis of their proximity to the exemplar site and that they represented a good example of what could otherwise have feasibly been built on the exemplar site. The sites were chosen on the basis of no other characteristics than that they represented nearby conventional residential schemes of a decent quality, likely to appeal to broadly the same market sector (in terms of price) as the exemplar scheme.

A major problem in finding suitable case studies was the reluctance of developers to participate in the study. To form comparators for the four exemplar schemes, suitable 'conventional' schemes were identified in each case but two of their developers later refused to participate in the study. Two hypothetical, standard development schemes were created and costed in the two locations that were left without 'conventional' sites.

There were several reasons for developers' unwillingness to participate, the main one being confidentiality. There was also a fear of being held up as an example of bad design. The 'conventional' sites are put forward as reasonable examples of conventional development with standardised layout practices. Their only shared characteristic is that, broadly, they are either not PPG3-compliant to the same extent as the exemplars or that they do not exhibit the innovative or best practice design principles, set out in the methodology above, to the same extent as the exemplar examples.

It is also worth noting that in the areas studied there was an increasing scarcity of non-PPG3 compliant, standard sites to act as conventional examples. Development, in the South-East and other southern parts of the country at least, is increasingly characterised by PPG3-type design principles.

3.3 Dealing with externalities

One reason put forward for the lack of comparable studies of value between good design and standard design quality is the fact that it is difficult to separate the differences in value that are due to design and those that are due to other factors. These other factors may include, among other things, access to schools, access to transport, access to other amenities, etc. Some research studies have attempted to account for these externalities through sophisticated statistical techniques such as hedonic mix adjusting methods and the validity of this methodology is addressed in the literature review section of this study.

For the purposes of this study, we originally proposed to identify matched pairs of 'exemplar' sites and 'conventional' sites with as near identical external characteristics as possible. The impact of externalities would then be removed in two ways:

1. through eliminating as many of the differences between sites' locations as possible
2. by measuring the impact of development on a homogenous product, namely land, rather than trying to assess the difference in value between exogenous units

An initial attempt was made to eliminate site differences through the utilisation of geographical information systems. However, it was found that there are simply not enough new build schemes of sufficient size in comparable locations to yield comparators on this basis.

A revised alternative method of excluding the impact of external influences on value was required. Instead, conventional developments in the same area but sometimes in slightly different types of location were chosen. By using a valuation approach to assess the gross development value of all schemes, the influence of different external factors on each scheme was then eliminated. This was done by asking experienced valuers, active in the local market-place, to assess each scheme as if it were on the same site as each of the exemplar schemes. In this way, like-for-like comparisons were obtained. The only variable that differed between each matched pair was the design and layout.

During the course of the research, two of the developers of conventional, comparator schemes decided to withdraw from the study. These schemes (at Chelmsford and Aylesbury) were replaced by the creation of a hypothetical scheme in each area. These hypothetical sites contained similar characteristics to the sites already selected (to provide a grounding in reality). A cost model of these sites was then created by Davis Langdon & Everest (DL&E) to emulate a typical, conventional local scheme.

The focus of this study on residual value per area of land, as opposed to unit value or value per square foot of unit, provided a common basis of measurement for all the sites. It was also a method by which they could all validly be compared. This negated the need to make adjustments or account for variations in the charateristics of the units on which value was measured. Instead, the residual value could be specified on a homogenous, uniform product (land) which differed only by the location of each matched pair. Even this broader, regional difference between the matched pairs could be eliminated by indexation using an appropriate index of regional building land values, if required.

3.4 Measuring and quantifying the sites

3.4.1 Site area

It became apparent during the course of this study that different developers measure site area in different ways. It was therefore necessary to standardise the measurement of sites in order to determine costs and values by land area on a like-for-like basis.

It was decided that the standard measure should be the total land area that would have to be bought by the developer in order to complete the development but excluding:

- any areas of major infrastructure such as bypasses and any associated landscaping, major distributor roads, etc
- land for section 106 development such as social housing, schools, pavilions, etc
- public open space including verges, footpaths not adjacent to roads (not pavements), cycle paths, village greens, recreation grounds, parks and other open space

Each scheme was measured using online Ordnance Survey (OS) maps or by digitising detailed OS site plans where the OS map was not available online. Where site boundaries were divided by roads, measurement was made up to the centre of the carriageway unless there was no current or future development on the other side of the road, in which case the whole carriageway was included.

While these measures may not always accord with what was done in practice on a site, it ensured that every scheme has been measured in the same way.

3.4.2 Layout type

The layout characteristics of each scheme were observed and described. Empirical measurement of the proportion of site land area utilised for different uses was also made. These uses included:

- public open space
- peripheral and feeder roads
- access roads and cul-de-sacs
- public driveways, parking courtyards and community space
- private driveways
- garages
- private gardens
- houses and flats

The proportion of land used for each of the above was intended to give a clearly quantified picture of the different nature of each scheme.

3.4.3 Appearance

Visits were made to each site and records made of the appearance of buildings and the site in general. Marketing material was also gathered to give a picture of internal layouts, appearance and finishes. In the case of the hypothetical schemes, detailed specifications, appearance and layout were devised.

3.5 Measuring costs

The building and marketing costs of each scheme were measured and assessed by Davis Langdon & Everest (DL&E) in extensive site visits and interviews with developers. In the case of the hypothetical sites, detailed development cost models were utilised in order to determine the cost to the developer of building and marketing a site.

The methodologies employed are detailed in Appendix 2, which contains the DL&E report.

The principle used in all the costings was that they should include all external works required to develop the plots, professional fees, sales and marketing expenses. The costs were deliberately compiled to exclude the costs of strategic site infrastructure such as remedial works and major roads, bypasses, road screening, etc. It also excluded the costs of any section 106 and 278 works as well as funding costs and central, company overhead contributions.

Costs were stated at March 2002 price levels, having been adjusted using cost indicators, where appropriate. The costs reflect the locality of each pair of projects and were not adjusted on a regional or local basis. The cost levels all assume the completion of the scheme as a single phase for sale in March 2003.

3.6 Measuring value

Little research has been conducted to ascertain the relative economic value of good design for the developer. This was specifically addressed by looking at the value of the whole scheme, rather than individual units (and by looking at the total development costs that might be involved) in order to determine economic value to the developer. The reasoning behind this approach was that it eliminated some of the effects of externalities and looked at commercial value rather than value to the end-user, the owner-occupier.

Approaches that have been used in other studies (for example, Eppli and Tu, *Valuing the new urbanism*, Urban Land Institute, 2001) have looked at value from the point of view of the open-market value:

- of individual units
- traded by, and to, owner-occupiers
- over time

The disadvantage of this approach was that it does not illustrate the value (or otherwise) of design to the developer (either an organisation or individual) who will actually be responsible for building the units (to any given design standard). It is developers, not owner-occupiers, who will determine whether certain design practices are put in place or not.

The examination of individual unit values also created problems of comparison between units, which varied greatly when ownership patterns and other factors differed. Attempts to adjust for these factors through hedonic mix adjusting were seen as inadequate because they could never account for every possible influence on value. Similarly, the choice of factors for which adjustment was made was, at best, subjective and often arbitrary. Details of the calculations made in this study are contained in Appendix 5.

A further problem was that other studies have used real transaction data to determine value differences. This was dangerous because the type and nature of properties in these transaction samples alter over time so it has not been possible to compare like with like at every stage. It was considered that there was no advantage in knowing that house type A sold for x and house type B sold for $x + y$ if the two could not be validly compared and/or they were sold at different times.

Likewise the examination of price growth failed to account for externalities that may have been due to factors such as differential economic performance between localities, the presence of nearby blight, changes in infrastructure and other external causes which may have been difficult either to account for or eliminate.

Another possible method of approaching this research would have been to use a contingent valuation method. This would have involved appraising an 'exemplar' site on which best practice housing had been built but then assuming that it had been built to a 'standard' specification, layout and design. The resulting hypothetical value could then have been compared with the actual values achieved on the best practice site and conclusions could have been drawn. This approach would have been valid to an extent (and indeed would have been very similar to the approach that was actually used where the conventional sites were hypothetical) but it was felt that such a completely hypothetical approach would not have been entirely credible to all observers.

The total development value of all the residential units in the schemes under study was assessed. In order to do this, a variety of local estate agents, valuers and development sales experts were contacted and asked to value each unit in every scheme. This method was imperative in the case of the hypothetical examples in any case but also had the advantage of eliminating any need to adjust revenues over time as all valuations were made for March 2002.

This valuation method relied on the skill and judgement of valuers who were making a subjective and hypothetical assessment. Care was taken to ensure that the valuers used were highly experienced in the field and in the local area with experience of either selling on the scheme or valuing similar schemes. In addition, at least two, and often three, opinions of value were sought from different valuers in

each case. The results were checked for anomalies and the average of all valuations for each unit was used.

In the case of the hypothetical examples, the schemes were carefully put together to reflect real, newly built properties that actually exist in the location in question. Consequently, the valuers were valuing unit types for which they had real comparables and real-life experience.

3.7 Assessing commercial value

The assessment of the commercial value to a developer of the scheme was made by:

1. taking the total gross value of the residential units only, as described above
2. subtracting the costs of developing the plots on which the units stand, building the units, finishing and marketing them according to the criteria set out above
3. analysing this on a per hectare of standardised land measurement

It is important to note that the resulting residual sums in each case never would have been representative of land value. They would be representative of sums available to the developer to cover both land costs and central corporate overheads as well as to be available as developer margin and profit (or loss) on the site.

4.0 Research results and discussion

4.1 Commercial value

With such a small sample, the headline results were inevitably inconclusive inasmuch as they neither prove nor disprove that innovative design and layout improve developer value. The methodology piloted in this report is itself a significant contribution to understanding values.

Of the four locations studied, three exemplar schemes yielded higher residual values than the conventional schemes and one yielded poorer residual values to the developer. In this one case, the difference in the residual value per hectare of land was less than 5%. Only in one scheme (Surbiton exemplar) was there a clear and definitively enhanced added value in the exemplar scheme. Here, residual value was enhanced by more than 15% over and above the standard scheme. In the exemplars at Bishop's Stortford and Chelmsford, both schemes' values appeared to be enhanced by the nature of their design (by 7.5% and 10.3% respectively).

Table 4.1: Residual value per area of land

Scheme	Location	Residual value per: Hectare	*Acre*	Difference to matched pair in same location
A	Surbiton – exemplar	£12.4m	*£5.0m*	+15.3%
B	Surbiton – conventional	£10.7m	*£4.3m*	–13.3%
C	Bishop's Stortford – exemplar	£4.6m	*£1.9m*	+7.5%
D	Bishop's Stortford – conventional	£4.3m	*£1.7m*	–6.9%
E	Chelmsford – exemplar	£3.8m	*£1.6m*	+10.3%
F	Chelmsford – conventional	£3.5m	*£1.4m*	–9.3%
G	Aylesbury – exemplar	£3.5m	*£1.4m*	–4.7%
H	Aylesbury – conventional	£3.7m	*£1.5m*	+5.0%

Source: FPDSavills

The following commentary provides some analysis as to what might be behind these differences in residual values.

4.2 Scheme characteristics

The tables in Appendix 3 contain the detailed characteristics of all the sites which help to explain the different schemes' performances. The differences between all the schemes are many, sometimes subtle and certainly varied. Not all of the exemplar examples are by any means similar, and even the standard examples vary from each other substantially.

4.2.1 Site size

Determining the size of each site in the study proved to be one of the most challenging aspects of this work. It would appear that the method by which

Research results and discussion

4.0

developers measure their sites is by no means standard and varies quite substantially. Some appear to be very conservative in their measurements (perhaps to raise the apparent density on the site) while others include every piece of land bought in order to facilitate the development.

It became apparent that the method by which each and every site was to be measured needed to be standardised. The standardised measurement is similar to that outlined in PPG3 but without distinguishing between children's playgrounds and other public open space. When measured this way, the schemes studied vary in size from under 1.5 hectares (under 4 acres) to over 7 hectares (over 18 acres).

The sample contains a wide variety of site sizes ranging from small stand-alone schemes through small phases on large schemes, big phases on larger schemes through to large standalone sites.

Table 4.2: Site size, by location

Scheme	Location	Total area		Standardised area		Developer's figure	
		Hectares	*Acres*	Hectares	*Acres*	Hectares	*Acres*
A	Surbiton – exemplar	9.1	*22.6*	7.3	*18.0*	8.3	*20.5*
B	Surbiton – conventional	4.4	*10.9*	3.9	*9.7*	4.9	*12.2*
C	Bishop's Stortford – exemplar	2.7	*6.7*	2.6	*6.4*	3.1	*7.5*
D	Bishop's Stortford – conventional	1.5	*3.8*	1.5	*3.7*	1.5	*3.7*
E	Chelmsford – exemplar	4.1	*10.1*	3.5	*8.6*	3.5	*8.7*
F	Chelmsford – conventional	4.2	*10.4*	3.8	*9.4*	N/A	*N/A*
G	Aylesbury – exemplar	1.8	*4.6*	1.8	*4.4*	1.9	*4.6*
H	Aylesbury – conventional	2.9	*7.3*	2.3	*5.8*	N/A	*N/A*

Source: FPDSavills

There appears to be no clear-cut relationship between how big a site is and whether innovative design is profitable or not. The sample size is insufficient to determine whether the size of the site itself is an important factor in determining the commercial performance of different types of design on the site studied. It is notable, however, that the clearest cut example of added development value was found on the biggest scheme. This may be because a large scheme has the biggest opportunity to really create its own sense of place while smaller schemes are more prone to the influence of other externalities and even other developments on adjacent sites.

It could be that the crucial factor is not size, *per se*, but the extent to which a scheme is self-contained. It is notable, for example, that the conventional scheme at Bishop's Stortford is small but it is self-contained and distinctive. Due to the characteristics of the location at Chelmsford, on the other hand, there are fewer differences between the hypothetical, conventional scheme and the exemplar scheme. They are not separated or distinct but both conform to very similar layouts and both are *Essex Design Guide* compliant.

It is possible that the image of place that has been created by the exemplar schemes in each case has influenced the value of adjacent conventional schemes. This possibility reveals a possible flaw in the methodology. Because all the conventional schemes were valued as if they were in the same location (although not on precisely the same site) as the exemplar schemes, an important component of design value may not be illustrated. This research will not pick up the possible added value to a place that innovative design might bring.

It is possible that some of the conventional schemes might benefit from being located adjacent to a successful exemplar scheme and achieve higher values than they might otherwise achieve in other surroundings. There may be future methodology revisions and designs that could overcome or even test this factor, perhaps to measure how an exemplar scheme might improve locally held perceptions of a new address, notably where it forms the frontage to the perimeter road for more standardised estate-type development behind.

4.2.2 Site density

Density is central to discussions on design and layout and is key to PPG3 but it is often poorly understood and crudely applied. It became apparent, within the parameters of this research, that density could be substantially affected by measurement norms and, even when measurement is standardised, can yield some surprising results.

It was clear that different schemes were built at different densities, for a variety of reasons. The conventional planning measure of density, used in PPG3, is in terms of units per hectare. By this measure, and using the standard site measurement that excludes public open space but includes access and minor perimeter roads, there was a range of site densities — from 16.2 units per hectare (6.5 per acre) to 43.3 units per hectare (17.5 per acre).

Table 4.3 shows the unit density per hectare and per acre for each of the sites studied. It shows a surprisingly wide range of densities between sites and, most surprisingly perhaps, between the exemplar sites. In fact, two of the exemplar sites (Bishop's Stortford and Chelmsford) turned out not to be PPG3-compliant in this respect because they had less than 30 units per hectare.

Table 4.3: Density: units per hectare (acre)

Scheme	Location	No. of units per: Hectare	*Acre*
A	Surbiton – exemplar	43.3	*17.5*
B	Surbiton – conventional	29.5	*11.9*
C	Bishop's Stortford – exemplar	22.3	*9.0*
D	Bishop's Stortford – conventional	16.2	*6.5*
E	Chelmsford – exemplar	27.6	*11.2*
F	Chelmsford – conventional	26.5	*10.7*
G	Aylesbury – exemplar	41.3	*16.7*
H	Aylesbury – conventional	32.5	*13.2*

Source: FPDSavills

It is interesting to note that, although all the conventional schemes are of lower density than their matched pairs, some are of higher density than other exemplar schemes elsewhere. It is noticeable that the density of units per hectare is over twice as high for the Surbiton exemplar (scheme A) than for its matched pair. This unit density was achieved by building apartments on the site and it reflects the fact that this location is among the most urban of all the examples. Achieving similar densities by building apartments on the scale of scheme A would simply not be an appropriate option in most of the other locations. It seems certain that it is this very high density that has contributed to the high residual values seen at the scheme A site.

In this respect, PPG3 can be the developer's ally by allowing a higher number of units to be built on a site than might otherwise have been the case in the past. This will enable unit production to rise on individual sites. Whether this would lead to higher overall production of units is subject to other factors such as land availability and is a potential subject for further research.

There is also a balance to be sought between density and the perceived quality of a place. The Surbiton exemplar (scheme A) arguably achieved this balance by combining dense and efficient terraced housing and apartments with large areas of open space. This made for an attractive location coupled with very efficient land use. It is worth noting the urban nature of such a solution compared to what might be possible on edge of town sites. Also, the size of the scheme, with its availability of large open spaces, may be critical in successfully achieving these densities without overly damaging market value. In this instance, the units in scheme A were worth slightly less per square metre than its matched conventional scheme, B. It was the higher number of square metres of built space accommodated in each hectare that made the big difference in residual land value.

Table 4.4: Site coverage, by location

Scheme	Location	Total area of development: ft^2	Coverage of housing units: ft^2
A	Surbiton – exemplar	785,393	442,786
B	Surbiton – conventional	424,172	188,266
C	Bishop's Stortford – exemplar	280,747	93,947
D	Bishop's Stortford – conventional	159,991	68,243
E	Chelmsford – exemplar	374,038	121,166
F	Chelmsford – conventional	409,916	121,916
G	Aylesbury – exemplar	192,991	59,690
H	Aylesbury – conventional	251,538	73,364

Source: FPDSavills

4.2.3 Development density

Development density differs from site density in that it describes something about the volume of houses built as well as the numbers built for each area of land. Development density is expressed as a ratio. The ratio is a product of the number of square metres (or square feet) of gross internal floor area divided by the number of square metres (or square feet) of site area.

Table 4.5: Density: gross internal area (gia) as percentage of site area

Scheme	Location	Development density ratio
A	Surbiton – exemplar	0.564
B	Surbiton – conventional	0.444
C	Bishop's Stortford – exemplar	0.335
D	Bishop's Stortford – conventional	0.427
E	Chelmsford – exemplar	0.324
F	Chelmsford – conventional	0.298
G	Aylesbury – exemplar	0.310
H	Aylesbury – conventional	0.292

Source: FPDSavills

While this figure alone is unable to describe how 'clustered' the development is, in most cases, the exemplar sites achieved higher build ratios than the conventional schemes. The exception was the Bishop's Stortford conventional scheme, D, which achieved high development density ratios by putting rooms in the loft and thereby, effectively, building to three storeys.

Scheme A illustrates that raising building height is the most effective way to achieve higher development density. Again, there is an issue with how appropriate taller forms might be in all rural, suburban and urban situations.

4.2.4 Land use

One of the clearest differences that could be measured between schemes was the different proportion of land use in each. An analysis of land use differentials was possibly the single most important tool to distinguish the different nature of design and layout between schemes. The tables in Appendix 3 show the proportion of land taken up by different land uses.

It can be seen that sites with relatively high residual values in relation to their matched pairs also appeared to have high proportions of public open space in relation to the overall size of the site.

4.2.5 Unit size

In nearly all cases, exemplar schemes had smaller unit sizes than the conventional schemes. This may be because higher densities have placed more emphasis on the size of the public realm rather than the size of the private realm.

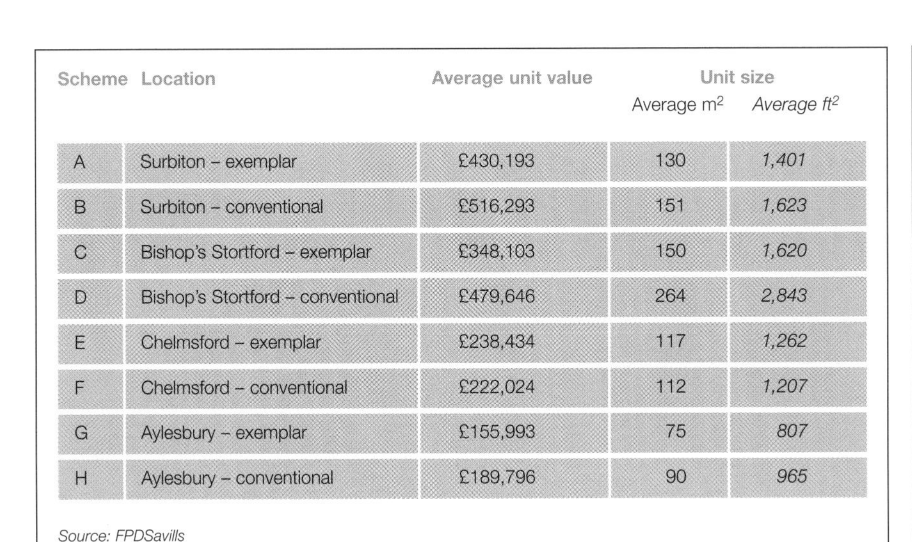

Scheme	Location	Average unit value	Unit size Average m²	Average ft²
A	Surbiton – exemplar	£430,193	130	*1,401*
B	Surbiton – conventional	£516,293	151	*1,623*
C	Bishop's Stortford – exemplar	£348,103	150	*1,620*
D	Bishop's Stortford – conventional	£479,646	264	*2,843*
E	Chelmsford – exemplar	£238,434	117	*1,262*
F	Chelmsford – conventional	£222,024	112	*1,207*
G	Aylesbury – exemplar	£155,993	75	*807*
H	Aylesbury – conventional	£189,796	90	*965*

Source: FPDSavills

Table 4.6: Size of units

Generally speaking, a bigger unit will sell for more than its smaller counterpart in the other matched pair. However, the residual value calculations in this report show that this increased value does not always make up for the more land-hungry nature of a larger building.

4.3 Costs

Build costs are generally considered by housebuilders to be a very important component of the house building process. There are few developers whose interest is not closely focused on this element and some devote considerable time, effort and research to finding ways of reducing it.

This is perhaps misplaced in view of the fact that this study found that enhancing unit values has a far bigger impact on developer profit than reducing costs. Table 4.7 shows the effect of

- reducing costs by 10%
- increasing revenue (GDV) by 10% on each of the case study sites

Cost reductions had the effect of increasing the residual value per hectare by between 4 and 8%. Increasing the value of units had a far bigger impact on potential margins, increasing the residual value per acre by between 14 and 18%.

While this study's sample is too small to prove that good design necessarily adds value to residential units, the GDV per hectare on all but one of the exemplar sites was higher than the conventional comparator. This indicates the possible value of further research and development to find ways of increasing the gross development value per hectare rather than concentrating solely on costs. We believe this merits further investigation.

Table 4.7: Percentage increase in residual value on each site

	A	B	C	D	E	F	G	H
Effect of reducing costs –10%	5.05	4.16	6.83	8.09	7.21	6.96	8.40	6.81
Effect of increasing revenue +10%	15.05	14.16	16.83	18.09	17.21	16.96	18.40	16.81

Source: FPDSavills

Perhaps of significance here is the way in which developers look at their finances. Few nowadays look at the absolute profit made on a single site but most would look instead at return on capital employed in the form of an internal rate of return (IRR). This has an important impact on the ability of developers to discern how they are making their money, whether it is the act of building houses or whether it is developing land that is creating value on a site. The form of analysis used here has begun to suggest that it may be the latter. Further robust investigation needs to be undertaken on more sites in order to ascertain this.

Full details and analysis of build, site and marketing costs are contained in Appendix 2 but Table 4.8 summarises them.

Table 4.8: Total build costs

Scheme	Location	Build costs: £000 Per hectare *(acre)*	Per m² *(ft²)*
A	Surbiton – exemplar	6,260 *(2,533)*	1,110 *(103)*
B	Surbiton – conventional	4,467 *(1,808)*	1,006 *(93)*
C	Bishop's Stortford – exemplar	3,143 *(1,272)*	939 *(87)*
D	Bishop's Stortford – conventional	3,466 *(1,403)*	812 *(75)*
E	Chelmsford – exemplar	2,761 *(1,117)*	852 *(79)*
F	Chelmsford – conventional	2,418 *(979)*	812 *(75)*
G	Aylesbury – exemplar	2,941 *(1,190)*	950 *(88)*
H	Aylesbury – conventional	2,501 *(1,012)*	857 *(80)*

Source: FPDSavills

When measured on a per standardised hectare basis, the building costs of the exemplar schemes are usually, but not always, higher than the conventional schemes. The Surbiton exemplar scheme, A, cost nearly twice as much per hectare as its matched pair, reflecting the fact that it was built at approximately double the density. The exemplar cases at Chelmsford, E, and Aylesbury, G, both cost 18% more than the conventional match. It is interesting to note, however, that the exemplar scheme at Bishop's Stortford cost less to build per hectare than the conventional example there, despite the unit density being higher. This possibly reflects the high development density (or mass) of the conventional scheme.

4.4 Values

4.4.1 Unit values

The notion that higher density decreases value was not supported by this study. In two of the four cases, the value of the units in the higher density scheme was higher on a per square metre basis than the comparable lower-density schemes (in one case, substantially so). Clearly, there is a critical balance to be struck by the developer in maintaining unit values while increasing density. Some developers managed to achieve

Table 4.9: Value of units

Scheme	Location	Unit value	
		Average	Per m² *(ft²)*
A	Surbiton – exemplar	£430,193	£3,305 (*£307*)
B	Surbiton – conventional	£516,293	£3,424 (*£318*)
C	Bishop's Stortford – exemplar	£348,103	£2,313 (*£215*)
D	Bishop's Stortford – conventional	£479,646	£1,816 (*£169*)
E	Chelmsford – exemplar	£238,434	£2,033 (*£189*)
F	Chelmsford – conventional	£222,024	£1,980 (*£184*)
G	Aylesbury – exemplar	£155,993	£2,082 (*£193*)
H	Aylesbury – conventional	£189,796	£2,116 (*£197*)

Source: DL&E, FPDSavills

this while others did not. Striking this balance is the single most important issue in determining the commercial value of PPG3-compliant schemes for the developer. There is compelling evidence to advocate that quality design can achieve high value environments while at the same time increasing density. Build costs are relatively unimportant in achieving this if value can be maintained.

The value of an individual unit is not a good indication of the value of a scheme to a developer. Both conventional schemes B and D at Surbiton and Bishop's Stortford have average unit values that are considerably higher than the exemplars but the residual value to the developer per hectare of land is still higher because the unit densities are higher. Some developers on higher density schemes have achieved a higher price per square metre than the lower density comparator.

Conclusions

5.0

5.0 Conclusions

This work provides an important first step in beginning to assess the value of design in the commercial world of housing development. It has not provided any clear-cut results and could never be deemed to have selected and tested a representative sample. Nevertheless, it has raised important issues about how design is valued and has indicated how it may make a difference to developers' profitability.

The first of the broad issues raised by the research is what creates value in the first place. A model of housing value, developed by FPDSavills' Research Department illustrates that there are numerous components of housing value ranging from basic shelter qualities, through amenity value and luxury value to investment and even speculative value. Design can clearly impact on the quality of the shelter and the amenities that a house has, and certainly the extent to which it is deemed to be luxurious or desirable.

The study highlighted the extent to which one development, particularly those larger schemes studied, can affect local externalities. There can be a knock-on effect on the surrounding area affecting not only value but also the sense of place and how a locality is perceived. It was noticeable that the innovative design elements of one developer on some parts of a larger development area could influence the value of the more conventionally designed housing on another part of a site, even though that housing did not follow the same design principles.

Does this research begin to address the question of how a desirable location may be created? The endlessly quoted and much loved estate agents' and TV presenters' phrase, 'location, location, location' is usually put forward as emphasising the most important element of housing value. Leaving aside the macroeconomics, there is a series of factors, including the built form, which creates a sense of place in a given location. Some of the developers in this study have helped to show that it is possible to create a sense of place, and hence a new type of location, on a piece of land by employing certain design principles. These new places may be more desirable, and therefore more valuable, than their neighbours and may also be made more desirable and valuable than would otherwise have been possible had standard development house types and layouts been employed. There is a strong compulsion to undertake further research using the method developed in this study to confirm that which is presently only indicative.

Developers and researchers in other locations and other situations have also noticed that the creation of a distinct place can enhance value. This value enhancement can spread further than just the site in question. Neighbouring developers and landowners also benefit. Commercial developments of high quality on a large scale have pushed up neighbouring land values for both commercial and residential development; examples include Brindley Place in Birmingham and Canary Wharf in London. Within this study, the exemplar schemes at Surbiton and Chelmsford may have achieved this. Other developers on nearby sites may well be benefiting from the sense of place that these schemes have provided for the location.

When it comes to value *for a developer* as opposed to an owner-occupier, it may be more appropriate to talk about 'density, density, density'. The issues involved are complex but the rules of the game now seem to be to maximise unit values while increasing the number of units on the site to meet planners' requirements. It may be said that this has always been the developers' game plan but new design techniques, and indeed changing planning rules, have upped the stakes. Whereas previously a developer might have aimed for densities of between 25 and 30 per hectare (10 and 12 per acre), new planning and design technologies have changed the target to something more like 30–40 per hectare (12–16 per acre). In urban situations, these densities would be very much higher again. Values will only be maintained at these densities if design techniques become very much more sophisticated to maintain the attractiveness to occupiers.

Another question that this research raises is whether design can ever make a really big value difference in a supply-constrained market. The sites under study were all in high demand regions of south-eastern England. This region is particularly characterised by very low levels of new build in relation to increasing demand for housing. The number of new developments makes a very small impact on overall supply in those housing markets. In a supply-constrained scenario, it may be that design has less of an impact than where purchasers' choices are freer. The question perhaps is, where the supply of new homes meets demand, whether conventional designs would sell at a discount or whether enhanced design would sell at a premium.

The final, and perhaps most important, question is whether this research is really measuring value to the developer. The margin that the developer makes out of any scheme is still highly dependent on the price the developer paid for the land. Even huge residuals would mean nothing if the developer has to pay exceptionally high prices to secure the land. In cases where competition for land is high (as it is in much of the South-East), it is likely that any developer with a competitive advantage (whether it be through design or for any other reason) will have to pass much of that value on to the landowner. This is because they would need to use enhanced value as their bidding advantage in order to secure the site against competition in the first place. Only where developers are part of the longer term land acquisition, ownership and land development process are they more likely to benefit from any enhanced value of their design efforts. This is likely to favour more adventurous developers who can add value at the start of the development process through design and detailed master-planning and who are prepared to separate their building activity from this specialised, but potentially lucrative, task.

Ultimately, therefore, it is very likely that if, for any reason, there were to be a revolution in development values it would only prove advantageous to a developer while the developer's competition were unwilling or unable to make use of the advantage themselves. FPDSavills has already predicted that land values will be driven up during the next 5–10 years, primarily through development gains of increased density. If certain other design principles were also discovered to increase development value, no doubt these would find their way into land values as well.

Not all of the exemplar schemes selected are as dense as PPG3 recommends.

While it would appear that good design may have enhanced the schemes' commercial value, what this study begins to show is that good design becomes more and more essential to achieve the maximum value as schemes increase in density, over 30 units per hectare. Standard design and standard layouts will not work on high density developments. Increases in density must accompany increased attention to design quality: there are clear commercial rewards when this course is followed.

There are clearly many questions to be answered and new avenues for this research to go down. A geographically broader and increased sample would enable more vigorous testing of hypotheses. It is to be hoped that this study will show how sites, costs and values can be analysed and that more developers will be willing to offer their schemes for scrutiny.

Appendix 1.0

Literature review references

a1.0 Literature review references

Adams, D. (1994) *Urban planning and the development process*, London, UCL Press

Ball, M. (1983) *Housing policy and economic power: the political economy of owner-occupation*, London, Methuen

Bartlett School of Planning, CABE (2001) *The value of urban design*, London, Thomas Telford

Booth, P. (1982) 'Housing as a product: design guidance and residential satisfaction in the private sector', *Built Environment*, 8, No. 1, 20–24

Bramley, G., Bartlett, W. and Lambert, C. (1995) *Planning, the market and private housebuilding*, London, UCL Press

Carmona, M. (1999) 'Controlling the design of private sector residential development: an agenda for improving practice', *Environment and Planning B: Planning and Design*, 26, 807–833

Carmona, M. (2001) *Housing design quality: through policy, guidance and review*, London, E & FN Spon

Cheshire, P. & Sheppard, S. (1997) 'The welfare economics of land use regulation', research papers in spatial and environmental analysis No. 42, Department of Geography, London School of Economics

Cheshire, P. and Sheppard, S. (2000) 'Building on brown fields: the long term price we pay', *Planning in London*, 33, April/June, 34–36

Civic Trust (1999) *Brownfield housing – 12 years on*, London, Civic Trust

Colquhoun, I. and Fauset, P.G. (1991) *Housing design in practice*, Harlow, Longman Scientific and Technical

Conran Roche/Davis Langdon & Everest (1989) *Costs of residential development*, London, Conran Roche

Davison, I. (1991) Land values: part of the design equation, *Housebuilder*, March, 38–44

Davison, I. (1990) *Good design in housing*, London, House Builders Federation/Royal Institute of British Architects

Department of the Environment/Housing Research Foundation (1976) *Design guidance survey: report on a survey of local authority design guidance for private residential development*, London, Department of the Environment

Department of the Environment (Northern Ireland)/Department for Regional Development (2000) *Creating places: achieving quality in residential environments*, Department of the Environment, Northern Ireland

Department of the Environment, Transport and the Regions (1998a) *Places, streets and movement: a companion guide to Design Bulletin 32 — Residential roads and footpaths*, London, DETR

Department of the Environment, Transport and the Regions (1998b) *Planning and development briefs: a guide to better practice*, London, DETR

Department of the Environment, Transport and the Regions (2000) *Planning Policy Guidance Note 3: Housing*, Norwich, The Stationery Office

Department of the Environment, Transport and the Regions/Commission for Architecture and the Built Environment (2000) *By design, Urban design in the planning system: towards better practice*, London, Thomas Telford

Department of Transport, Local Government and the Regions/Commission for Architecture and the Built Environment (2001) *By design: better places to live*, London, Thomas Telford

Essex County Council (1973) *A design guide for residential areas*, Colchester, County Council of Essex

Essex Planning Officers Association (1997) *A design guide for residential and mixed use areas*, Essex, Essex Planning Officers Association

Goodchild, G. (1994) 'Housing design, urban form and sustainable development', *Town Planning Review*, 65 (2) 143–158

Goodchild, B. (1997) *Housing and the urban environment: a guide to house design, renewal and urban planning*, Oxford, Blackwell Science

Hall, A. (1990) *Generation of objectives for design control*, Chelmsford, Anglia College Enterprises Ltd

Hanson, J. (1999) *Decoding homes and houses*, Cambridge, Cambridge University Press

Hooper, A. & Nicol, C. (1999) 'The design and planning of residential development: standard house types in the speculative housebuilding industry', *Environment and Planning B: Planning and Design*, 26, 793–805

Hooper, A. & Nicol, C. (2000) 'Design practice and volume production in speculative housebuilding', *Construction Management and Economics*, 18, 295–310

Karn, V. (1992) 'British housing standards: time for a new approach?' in *Housing design — time for a new approach*, London, Housing Centre Trust

Karn, V. and Sheridan, L. (1994) *New homes in the 1990s: a study of design, space and amenity in housing association and private sector production*, University of Manchester/Joseph Rowntree Foundation

Leopold, E. and Bishop, D. (1983a) 'Design philosophy and practice in speculative housebuilding: Part 1', *Construction Management and Economics*, 1, 119–144

Leopold, E. and Bishop, D. (1983b) 'Design philosophy and practice in speculative housebuilding: Part 2', *Construction Management and Economics*, 1, 233–268

Llewelyn-Davies (1994) *Providing more homes in urban areas*, University of Bristol, SAUS Publications

Llewelyn-Davies (1998) *Sustainable residential quality: new approaches to urban living*, London, London Advisory Planning Committee

Llewelyn-Davies (1999) *Sustainable residential quality II: approach and method statement*, London, London Advisory Planning Committee

Llewelyn-Davies (2000a) *Sustainable residential quality: exploring the housing potential of large sites*, London, London Advisory Planning Committee

Llewelyn-Davies (2000b) *Urban design compendium*, London, English Partnerships/The Housing Corporation

Nicol, C. & Hooper, A. (1999) 'Contemporary change and the housebuilding industry: concentration and standardisation in production', *Housing Studies*, 14, No. 1, 57–76

Parfect, M. and Power, G. (1997) *Planning for urban quality: urban design in towns and cities*, London, Routledge

Planning Officers Society, Housebuilders Federation and DETR (1998) *Housing layouts — lifting the quality*, London, HBF

Popular Housing Forum (now Popular Housing Group) (1998) *Kerb appeal: the external appearance and site layout of new houses*, Winchester, Popular Housing Group

Punter, J. and Carmona, M. (1997) *The design dimension of planning: theory, content and best practice for design policies*, London, E & FN Spon

RICS (1996) *Quality of urban design: a study of the involvement of private property decision-makers in urban design*, London, Royal Institution of Chartered Surveyors

Rudlin, D. & Falk, N. (1995) *21st century homes: building to last*, York, Joseph Rowntree Foundation

Rudlin, D. & Falk, N. (1999) *Building the 21st century home: the sustainable urban neighbourhood*, Oxford, Architectural Press

Sim, D. (1993) *British housing design*, Harlow, Longman

Syms, P. (2001) *Releasing brownfields*, London, RICS Foundation

Syms, P. and Knight, P. (2000) *Building homes on used land*, London, RICS Books

Urban Task Force (1999) *Towards an urban renaissance*, London, E & FN Spon

Verhage, R. and Needham, B. (1997) 'Negotiating about the residential environment: it is not only money that matters', *Urban Studies*, 34, No. 12, 2053–2068

Worpole, K. (1999) *The value of architecture — design, economy and the architectural imagination*, RIBA Future Studies Series, London, RIBA

Appendix 2.0

Cost analysis by Davis Langdon & Everest

a2.0 Assessment of development costs

A2.1 Introduction

This section of the report discusses the objectives and scope of the analysis of housing development costs. The methodologies adopted for data collection, analysis and presentation are outlined. Issues associated with the analysis of the data and the results, which could have an influence on the overall outcome of the study, are also identified.

A2.2 Objective

The objective of this cost assessment is to establish benchmark development costs for each scheme using formats that facilitate direct comparison. The adjustment and analysis of the development cost data provides the basis on which an assessment of net development value and overall land value can be calculated. Issues that need to be addressed in preparing this analysis include:

- the establishment of a common data structure
- ensuring that the full scope of relevant development costs are captured for each project
- adjusting costs for time and location to enable direct comparisons to be made between matched pairs of developments

A2.3 Data collection

Construction and development cost data has been collected directly from a group of contributing housebuilding companies. Interviews were held with commercial managers, during which detailed cost and project information was collected. These meetings gave Davis Langdon & Everest's (DL&E's) researchers the opportunity to collect additional information related to market conditions and other variables that could potentially affect the overall development cost assessment.

No standard cost breakdown structure is available for use on private housing projects. The information collected for this project has, as a result, been provided in a number of formats, often related to the costs of individual trades or tranches of building materials. The researchers have re-categorised this information to permit direct comparison between projects.

The information provided by the developers is potentially very commercially sensitive. The team's awareness of this consideration has influenced the extent to which detailed analysis of the development costs information can be undertaken as follows:

- costs are reported on a scheme-wide basis; specific costs for individual dwelling types are not published
- costs are reported using indirect units of comparison (cost per square foot of gross internal floor area or cost per acre)

In two locations, it has not been possible to obtain detailed project and cost information for a pair of comparable projects. In these circumstances, models have been developed based on design information available in the public domain and comparable cost information derived from the rest of the sample. The issues associated with the preparation of the models are discussed further in section A2.5 below.

A2.4 Scope and structure of project cost data

In the preparatory analysis, cost data collected from each developer has been adjusted to include only cost centres that relate to the development cost of specific phases of development. For example, in order to facilitate comparison between schemes, costs of primary infrastructure and site development costs have been excluded. The following cost centres are included in the analysis:

- construction cost — building only
- construction costs — external works and services constructed as part of the development
- phase featured in the sample
- construction costs — preliminaries (contractor's on-site management resources)
- internal development costs including:
  - designers' fees, fees associated with planning and NHBC inspections, etc
  - internal marketing costs including show homes, sales staff costs and advertising, etc

Items excluded from the analysis include:

- remediation works
- site development costs beyond the boundary of the site/phase — this includes all section 106 and section 278 works associated with the development
- for larger schemes, where the sample comprises one or more phases of a larger development, this means that the costs of site preparation and strategic infrastructure works required to prepare the site for development are also excluded, as are communal facilities such as parks and shelter belts which benefit other phases of the scheme
- for smaller, or self-contained schemes, all infrastructure within the site boundary is included, on the basis that the extent of works required will be equivalent to that of a single phase on a larger housing development
- finance costs
- costs of head office overheads and profit

The exclusion of these items from the scope of the analysis does not affect the validity of the outcome. By removing site- and contractor-specific variables, such as those related to site conditions, infrastructure and planning requirements, and costs of development, capital costs based on common criteria can be directly compared. While this represents a simplification of the total cost equation, use of this assumption ensures that the analysis identifies relationships between scheme design, density building cost and development value. In particular, the exclusion of planning gain costs, etc removes a significant source of site-specific variation from the data set.

A2.5 Analysis of the data

A2.5.1 Normalisation

The primary objective of the analysis is to provide consistent, comparable development cost information for input into the overall assessment of development value. The data is also presented in a range of formats to facilitate the comparison of schemes in the sample.

Adjustments required to ensure that the cost information is comparable are as follows:

- **Inflation** — development costs have been brought to a common datum (March 2002) using DL&E's published tender price index. The adjustments used were verified using information provided by feedback from the developers' commercial managers
- **Location** — cost differentials between locations have been updated to levels current in March 2002 using location factors published by the Building Cost Information Service of the RICS
- **Common units of comparison** — gross internal floor area and overall site area have been used as the units of comparison

A2.5.2 Development of cost models

It has not been possible to obtain cost information for two schemes in the sample. As an alternative, cost models have been prepared to provide the basis for the comparison. The key features of the cost models are:

- the size, layout and mix of dwellings is based on a specific, directly comparable scheme
- costs are derived from appropriate schemes elsewhere in the sample
- cost models reflect differences in quantities related to key cost drivers for each house type
- models were developed for each house type in a scheme

The models were developed from drawn information and other marketing material available in the public domain. While the research team acknowledges that the models are generic and cannot account for all minor variations in detailed design, these variations only have a limited cost impact. Given the circumstances of the study, the models represent the most effective method of obtaining cost information with an acceptable level of accuracy.

In compiling the models, DL&E have also taken into account differences in external works content — particularly road and sewer layouts. The assessment of other development costs (fees, marketing costs, etc) is based on a review of the proportion of costs recorded on the other projects in the sample.

A2.5.3 Presentation of the data

The results of the analysis are published in three formats.

- **Total cost per square foot of gross internal floor area**. This analysis provides a direct comparison of development cost based on the average building cost for each scheme. A number of variables will affect these costs, including some which are site-specific rather than related to the design of the house type such as:
  - extent of substructure works related to local ground conditions
  - extent of external works, which are affected by both the extent and quality of works in the public domain, and by the development density of the scheme

  The inclusion of these costs makes it difficult to identify differences in the construction costs related to specification. These can be identified more clearly in an analysis of superstructure costs
- **Superstructure only costs per square foot of gross internal floor area**. This analysis eliminates the variables of substructure and external works and enables a direct comparison to be made between the costs associated with the build quality of the particular dwelling mix

  This comparison excludes the key element of the external works, which clearly contribute to value through the provision of a high quality public realm. External works need to be assessed using a different unit of comparison — site area — to provide meaningful results
- **Total costs per acre**. This analysis enables the effect of the key variable of development density to be accounted for. External works costs can be compared directly on the basis of the site area rather than gross internal floor area (gifa)

A2.6 Results

Table A2.1 sets out the total development costs for the eight schemes in the sample. The projects are organised as matched pairs in accordance with the study methodology outlined elsewhere in this report. The costs of each matched pair of schemes have been brought to a common datum related to their location. Table A2.2 uses a similar format to present superstructure-only costs.

Market conditions and price levels in the locations of schemes C to H are similar and these projects can be compared more or less directly. However, market conditions and other factors affecting costs of projects in south-west London mean that the costs of schemes A and B are subject to a 5% premium compared to others in the sample.

Table A2.1: Total summary construction costs

	Scheme A		Scheme B		Scheme C		Scheme D	
	South-west London				East Hertfordshire			
Site area (acres)	20.51		12.18		5.96		3.65	
Development area (ft²)	442,786		188,266		93,947		68,243	
Development density	0.496		0.355		0.362		0.429	
Development cost	£/ft²	%	£/ft²	%	£/ft²	%	£/ft²	%
Foundations/ground slabs	6.28	6.09	3.78	4.05	5.99	6.86	3.76	4.99
Masonry	17.52	17.00	11.32	12.12	9.72	11.15	10.49	13.90
Carpentry/windows/doors	9.36	9.08	9.45	10.12	9.83	11.27	12.10	16.04
Roof coverings	2.60	2.53	3.82	4.09	3.45	3.95	2.62	3.48
Joinery, fixtures and fittings	3.27	3.17	2.13	2.28	8.04	9.22	1.86	2.46
Finishes	13.52	13.11	9.88	10.58	8.38	9.61	7.52	9.96
Kitchen installation	4.88	4.74	3.57	3.82	4.45	5.11	3.26	4.32
Services	11.60	11.26	9.91	10.60	6.52	7.48	8.73	11.57
Preliminaries	13.61	13.20	19.56	20.93	8.54	9.79	7.64	10.13
Site preparation	0.92	0.89	0.49	0.52	0.00	0.00	0.36	0.47
External works	6.79	6.59	7.74	8.29	7.67	8.80	4.78	6.33
Drainage and below ground services	3.03	2.94	4.56	4.88	3.88	4.45	3.63	4.81
Internal development costs (fees, planning legal, NHBC, inspections, customer care)	9.69	9.40	7.21	7.71	10.72	12.29	8.71	11.54
Total Build Cost	103.08	100.00	93.42	100.00	87.20	100.00	75.44	100.00

	Scheme E		Scheme F		Scheme G		Scheme H	
	Essex				Buckinghamshire			
Site area (acres)	8.70		8.65		4.56		5.51	
Development area (ft²)	121,166		121,916		59,690		73,364	
Development density	0.320		0.324		0.301		0.306	
Development cost	£/ft²	%	£/ft²	%	£/ft²	%	£/ft²	%
Foundations/ground slabs	10.04	12.68	5.54	7.34	7.18	8.14	5.59	7.02
Masonry	11.52	14.56	10.09	13.36	9.58	10.85	10.49	13.17
Carpentry/windows/doors	10.42	13.16	11.59	15.35	10.82	12.25	12.61	15.84
Roof coverings	4.67	5.90	3.11	4.12	3.38	3.82	2.87	3.60
Joinery, fixtures and fittings	2.24	2.83	1.42	1.89	1.70	1.93	1.45	1.82
Finishes	7.22	9.12	5.75	7.62	6.43	7.28	5.86	7.36
Kitchen installation	4.50	5.69	1.79	2.37	2.55	2.89	2.11	2.65
Services	7.63	9.65	8.56	11.34	10.10	11.44	8.88	11.15
Preliminaries	7.96	10.06	7.16	9.49	8.34	9.45	8.91	11.20
Site preparation	0.00	0.00	0.00	0.00	0.00	0.00	0.00	0.00
External works	3.82	4.83	7.19	9.52	11.68	13.23	8.56	10.75
Drainage and below ground services	2.89	3.65	4.60	6.09	6.26	7.09	3.13	3.93
Internal development costs (fees, planning legal, NHBC, inspections, customer care)	6.23	7.88	8.68	11.50	10.26	11.62	9.16	11.50
Total Build Cost	79.13	100.00	75.48	100.00	88.27	100.00	79.62	100.00

- The table details average building costs for all dwellings on eight housing schemes in south-east England. Costs are given on the basis of cost per square foot of gross internal floor area
- Costs are stated at March 2002 price levels, and reflect the costs associated with the locality of each pair of projects. The price level reflects the completion of the housing as a single phase for sale in March 2002
- The costs in this table include all project specific development costs associated with each scheme, including all external works required to develop the plot, professional fees and sales and marketing expenses
- The analysis does not include costs of strategic site infrastructure or section 106 and 278 works. The analysis also excludes funding costs and overhead contributions

The results of the analysis summarised in Tables A2.1 and A2.2 show that the four urban design exemplar schemes are consistently more expensive to construct than their conventional equivalents. The only exceptions are the superstructure building only costs associated with schemes G and H in Essex. The overall cost differential is set out in Tables A2.3 and A2.4.

Table A2.2: Summary superstructure construction costs

	Scheme A		Scheme B		Scheme C		Scheme D	
	South-west London				East Hertfordshire			
Site area (acres)	20.51		12.18		5.96		3.65	
Development area (ft²)	442,786		188,266		93,947		68,243	
Development density	0.496		0.355		0.362		0.429	
Development cost	£/ft²	%	£/ft²	%	£/ft²	%	£/ft²	%
Masonry	17.52	27.92	11.32	22.61	9.72	19.30	10.49	22.52
Carpentry/windows/doors	9.36	14.92	9.45	18.87	9.83	19.50	12.10	25.99
Roof coverings	2.60	4.15	3.82	7.62	3.45	6.84	2.62	5.63
Joinery, fixtures and fittings	3.27	5.21	2.13	4.26	8.04	15.96	1.86	3.98
Finishes	13.52	21.54	9.88	19.74	8.38	16.63	7.52	16.14
Kitchen installation	4.88	7.78	3.57	7.13	4.45	8.83	3.26	7.00
Services	11.60	18.49	9.91	19.78	6.52	12.94	8.73	18.74
Superstructure, fittings and finishes costs	62.76	100.00	50.09	100.00	50.40	100.00	46.57	100.00

	Scheme E		Scheme F		Scheme G		Scheme H	
	Essex				Buckinghamshire			
Site area (acres)	8.70		8.65		4.56		5.51	
Development area (ft²)	121,166		121,916		56,690		73,364	
Development density	0.320		0.324		0.301		0.306	
Development cost	£/ft²	%	£/ft²	%	£/ft²	%	£/ft²	%
Masonry	11.52	23.90	10.09	23.84	9.58	21.50	10.49	23.69
Carpentry/windows/doors	10.42	21.61	11.59	27.39	10.82	24.28	12.61	28.49
Roof coverings	4.67	9.69	3.11	7.35	3.38	7.58	2.87	6.47
Joinery, fixtures and fittings	2.24	4.65	1.42	3.37	1.70	3.82	1.45	3.28
Finishes	7.22	14.98	5.75	13.60	6.43	14.43	5.86	13.24
Kitchen installation	4.50	9.34	1.79	4.22	2.55	5.73	2.11	4.77
Services	7.63	15.84	8.56	20.24	10.10	22.67	8.88	20.06
Superstructure, fittings and finishes costs	48.19	100.00	42.31	100.00	44.56	100.00	44.27	100.00

- The table details average building costs for all dwellings on eight housing schemes in south-east England. Costs are given on the basis of cost per square foot of gross internal floor area
- Costs are stated at March 2002 price levels, and reflect the costs associated with the locality of each pair of projects. The price level reflects the completion of the housing as a single phase for sale in March 2002
- The costs in this table include costs associated with the superstructure, finishes and services of the houses in each scheme only. All below ground works, preliminaries and external works required to develop the plot, professional fees and sales and marketing expenses are excluded. This analysis makes it easier to identify differences in specification between each scheme. (Refer to Table 1 for the total costs)
- The analysis does not include costs of strategic site infrastructure or section 106 and 278 works. The analysis also excludes funding costs and overhead contributions

Table A2.3: Differential in total construction costs — total development cost

	Schemes A & B	Schemes C & D	Schemes E & F	Schemes G & H
Exemplar scheme (£/ft^2)	103.08	87.20	79.13	88.27
Conventional scheme (£/ft^2)	93.42	75.44	75.48	79.62
Differential (%)	90.6	86.5	95.4	90.2

Source: DL&E, FPDSavills

Table A2.4: Differential in total construction costs — superstructure costs only

	Schemes A & B	Schemes C & D	Schemes E & F	Schemes G & H
Exemplar scheme (£/ft^2)	62.76	50.40	48.19	44.56
Conventional scheme (£/ft^2)	50.09	46.57	42.31	44.27
Differential (%)	80.0	92.0	87.8	99.0

Source: DL&E, FPDSavills

The further analysis of the differentials between the costs of the matched pairs is set out in section A2.6.2, *Analysis of matched pairs*.

A2.6.1 Sources of variation in building costs

The comparison of the construction costs of low-rise residential schemes is relatively straightforward, as there is a limited number of variables that can affect the overall level of cost. The principal variables are detailed below.

- **Site conditions and foundations design**. The design and costs of foundations are generally influenced more by ground conditions than by the specific design, layout and massing of dwellings. Poor ground conditions can add significantly to construction costs. However, substructure costs are easily identified and can be isolated from the comparison if required, as they have been from Table A2.2
- **Efficiency of layout**. The efficiency of house layout effectively determines how much building superstructure is required to enclose each square foot of accommodation. More efficiently designed dwellings will, all other factors being equal, have relatively low external wall and roof costs. Although the differences can be marginal, the cost effect can be more significant due to the direct effect on the costs of masonry, carpentry and roof coverings, which account for a high proportion of overall construction costs. Other factors which affect building efficiency include the facts that:
  - larger dwellings tend to be slightly more efficient than smaller versions of the same layout
  - standard developer homes based on a square plan are particularly efficient
  - the introduction of rooms in the roof increases the overall efficiency of house layout and design

- **Specification of materials, fixtures and fittings**. The cost breakdown designed for this study enables significant variations in the cost of elements to be identified. Some of these differences will be due to specification variations, which may also affect development value. For the purposes of this study, it is not necessary to quantify differences between the detailed design of matched pairs, however, this analysis provides the opportunity to identify where developers of high cost/higher value properties are spending in response to consumer demand
- **Kitchens**. The square foot cost of kitchens and white goods is generally higher in smaller dwellings
- **External works**. The extent and mix of external treatments, and potential range of materials and specifications mean that external works also need to be clearly identified and isolated to enable direct comparison of house construction costs. External work costs, analysed on the basis of cost per square foot, are also affected by the density of development, with two factors in particular combining to affect the overall rate:
  - an increasing proportion of hard landscaping as schemes increase in density, resulting in higher costs
  - the reduction in square foot costs of external works generally on schemes with a high proportion of gross floor area to overall site area

These factors are illustrated in Table A2.5 which sets out the densities and costs (per square foot and per acre) for external works on each scheme.

Table A2.5: Summary costs of external works

	A	B	C	D	E	F	G	H
Density	0.496	0.355	0.362	0.429	0.320	0.324	0.301	0.306
Rate (£/ft²)	6.79	7.74	7.67	4.78	3.82	7.19	11.68	8.56
Rate (£/acre)	146,614	119,662	120,956	89,308	53,224	101,288	152,858	113,948

Source: DL&E, FPDSavills

Table A2.5 illustrates the range of costs recorded for external works, and the changing relationships between these costs related to the unit of comparison adopted.

A2.6.2 Analysis of matched pairs

This section of the report sets out a more detailed discussion of the costs of the projects, based on the data sets detailed in Tables A2.1 and A2.2.

1. Surbiton, south-west London

Schemes A & B are the only developments located in an urban setting. Situated in south-west London, these are the two most costly schemes in the sample, even when relative cost levels are taken into account. Schemes A & B are the only projects that feature apartments as part of the project. Scheme A is also the densest in the sample. The impact of density can be seen in the relatively low proportion of expenditure on external works, for a scheme that has the most extensive landscaping investment. (Cost of landscaping per acre is £146,614 compared to a normalised sample average of £108,916 per acre.)

Relatively high levels of capital expenditure on scheme A are focused on substructure (associated with undercroft car parking), masonry, joinery and finishes, reflecting a high level of specification throughout the scheme, which is likely to drive up overall development value. Scheme B costs are fairly similar to those of projects outside London. A very high proportion of the costs of this scheme is associated with preliminaries — which potentially could include items of unstated direct labour or the sourcing of materials. Table A2.2 sets out superstructure building works only costs for the sample of eight projects. Adjusted for location (£47.60 per ft^2), the costs of scheme B are very similar to those found on projects C to H. Notably, high levels of expenditure on this scheme are directed at internal finishes.

2. Bishop's Stortford, East Hertfordshire

Schemes C & D are both high quality developments located on estates on a rural/urban fringe. Both incorporate elements of PPG3, with dwellings in scheme C being built up to the street-line, and scheme D featuring houses with rooms in the roof. Both schemes are designed to a relatively high level of density when measured on the basis of the ratio of floor area to site area. However, the dwellings on both schemes are large and neither scheme meets the density targets set in PPG3.

Scheme C features houses strongly influenced by the vernacular design and also incorporates extensive hard landscaping. The cost breakdown in Table A2.1 shows that the costs of scheme C are relatively high — demonstrating that the construction of non-standard housing does involve a cost premium. From the analysis in Table A2.2, there is evidence of an across-the-board approach to investment in quality, with higher than average expenditure on joinery, fixtures and fittings, and finishes.

Scheme D features large four- and five-bed houses. Overall costs are relatively low, partly due to the large size of the dwellings and also due to the influence of rooms in the roof on the efficiency of the design and its use of building materials. Table A2.2 shows that there are particularly low levels of expenditure on roof coverings, joinery and kitchens. The low cost of roofing and kitchen fittings is often a result of these costs being amortised over an especially large floor area. The low cost of joinery and fittings may be as a result of some items being included in the carpentry section. Overall, the breakdown shows slightly higher expenditure on masonry and services — areas that directly affect building quality and occupant comfort respectively. Low external works costs can be associated with the simplicity of the cul-de-sac design concept and the high density (in terms of relative area, not number of dwellings) of the scheme.

3. Chelmsford, Essex

Schemes E & F are phases of development of a large site on a rural/urban fringe. The design of the layout of both developments is strongly influenced by principles laid out in the *Essex Design Guide*. The developments feature a mix of three- and four-bed dwellings. Only limited information has been provided for scheme E by the developer. The scheme features a wide variety of units in complex configurations. While overall scheme development costs, at £79/ft^2, are relatively low, the superstructure building costs, at £48/ft^2, are among the highest in the sample. High levels of expenditure are recorded on substructures, masonry, carpentry/windows/doors and the kitchen installation. Table A2.2 highlights this pattern of expenditure.

The construction costs for scheme F are based on the output of a generic model. It should be noted that the costs of substructure are also based on a generic solution as no site details or site-specific costs are available. If the substructure costs of schemes E & F were identical, then the overall construction cost of scheme F would be just over £80/ft^2, i.e. slightly higher than scheme E. This addition to total construction cost would have a significant impact on development value and funds available for land purchase. The external works costs for scheme F are the higher of the pair, related to costs of hard paving to shared driveways and some shared open space. In both schemes, extensive provision of shared open space, either in parks/greens, or in heavily landscaped pedestrian avenues, are excluded from the analysis, as these facilities are provided as part of the overall site infrastructure rather than as a site-specific amenity.

In the model, while absolute costs for scheme F, detailed in Table A2.2, are lower than for scheme E, the allocation between cost centres is consistent, with the exception of expenditure on the kitchen and services.

4. Aylesbury, Buckinghamshire

The costs of scheme H are based on the output of a model, with costs based on schemes within the sample. Table A2.2 shows that there is little difference between the costs of superstructure components of the model scheme and scheme G. The primary source of differential is in the external works and below ground services, where costs on scheme G are the highest in the sample, featuring substantial levels of investment in hard landscape, boundary walls, etc. The houses in scheme G are standard dwelling types with enhancements to masonry and roof specification.

Appendix 3.0

Characteristics of each site

Site A

Location	Surbiton, outer south-west London
Type	Exemplar. Real, existing site. Stand-alone scheme
Developer	St James Homes

Total size of site: (all the land the developer would have bought, including feeder and access roads but excluding major bypasses and distributor roads)	9.1 hectares (22.6 acres)
Standardised size of site: (as above but excluding public open space such as parks, greens, verges and recreation ground)	7.3 hectares (18.0 acres)
Developer's stated size of site: (where applicable)	8.3 hectares (20.5 acres)

Land use by size of footprint

Land use	As a percentage of total size
Public open space	20.3%
Peripheral and feeder roads, access roads and cul-de-sacs	13.4%
Public driveways, parking courtyards and shared space	1.6%
Private driveways	9.0%
Garages	0.4%
Private gardens	37.0%
Houses and flats	18.3%

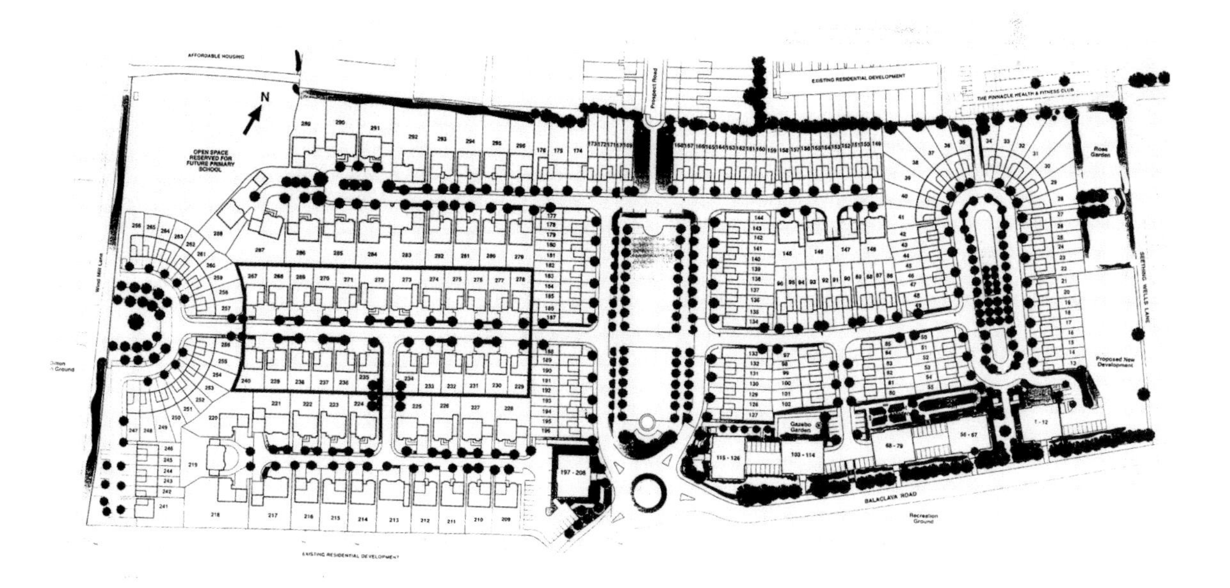

Number of units

Type	All:	5+ beds	4 beds	3 beds	2 beds	1 bed
Detached	63	38	25	—	—	—
Semi-detached	—	—	—	—	—	—
Terraced	175	—	175	—	—	—
Apartments	78	—	—	—	36	42
TOTAL	316	38	200	—	36	42

Number of habitable rooms	1,859
Number of bed spaces	1,740
Area of all residential buildings (gross internal area)	41,136 m^2 (442,786 ft^2)

Densities

	On the basis of Whole site area	Standardised site area
Dwellings (units) per hectare (acre)	35 (14)	43 (18)
Habitable rooms per hectare (acre)	203 (82)	255 (103)
Bed spaces per hectare (acre)	190 (77)	239 (97)
Plot ratio (coverage)		0.564

(Gross internal area built as proportion of site area)

Site B

Location	Surbiton, outer south-west London
Type	Conventional. Real, existing site. Large phase on larger scheme
Developer	Fairview

Total size of site: (all the land the developer would have bought, including feeder and access roads but excluding major bypasses and distributor roads)	4.4 hectares (10.9 acres)
Standardised size of site: (as above but excluding public open space such as parks, greens, verges and recreation ground)	3.9 hectares (9.7 acres)
Developer's stated size of site: (where applicable)	4.9 hectares (12.2 acres)

Land use by size of footprint

Land use	As a percentage of total size
Public open space	10.7%
Peripheral and feeder roads	15.1%
Access roads and cul-de-sacs	1.3%
Public driveways, parking courtyards and shared space	0.0%
Private driveways	9.7%
Garages	1.8%
Private gardens	42.3%
Houses and flats	19.3%

Number of units

Type	All:	5+ beds	4 beds	3 beds	2 beds	1 bed
Detached	44	26	18	—	—	—
Semi-detached	18	6	12	—	—	—
Terraced	42	2	40	—	—	—
Apartments	12	—	—	—	6	6
TOTAL	116	34	70	—	6	6

Number of habitable rooms	806
Number of bed spaces	751
Area of all residential buildings (gross internal area)	17,490 m^2 (188,266 ft^2)

Densities

	On the basis of Whole site area	Standardised site area
Dwellings (units) per hectare (acre)	26 (11)	30 (12)
Habitable rooms per hectare (acre)	183 (74)	205 (83)
Bed spaces per hectare (acre)	170 (69)	191 (77)
Plot ratio (coverage)		0.444

(Gross internal area built as proportion of site area)

Site C

Location	Bishop's Stortford, East Hertfordshire
Type	Exemplar. Real, existing site. Large, late phase on larger scheme
Developer	Countryside Properties

Total size of site: (all the land the developer would have bought, including feeder and access roads but excluding major bypasses and distributor roads)	2.6 hectares (6.5 acres)
Standardised size of site: (as above but excluding public open space such as parks, greens, verges and recreation ground)	2.6 hectares (6.4 acres)
Developer's stated size of site: (where applicable)	3.1 hectares (7.5 acres)

Land use by size of footprint

Land use	As a percentage of total size
Public open space	7.3%
Peripheral and feeder roads	17.4%
Access roads and cul-de-sacs, public driveways, parking courtyards and shared space	15.7%
Private driveways	1.1%
Garages	5.7%
Private gardens	33.3%
Houses and flats	19.5%

Number of units

Type	All:	5+ beds	4 beds	3 beds	2 beds	1 bed
Detached	18	4	13	1	—	—
Semi-detached	31	—	14	15	2	—
Terraced	9	—	—	9	—	—
Apartments	0	—	—	—	—	—
TOTAL	58	4	27	25	2	—

Number of habitable rooms	354
Number of bed spaces	333
Area of all residential buildings (gross internal area)	32,049 m^2 (334,979 ft^2)

Densities

	On the basis of Whole site area	Standardised site area
Dwellings (units) per hectare (acre)	22 (9)	22 (9)
Habitable rooms per hectare (acre)	134 (54)	136 (55)
Bed spaces per hectare (acre)	127 (51)	129 (52)
Plot ratio (coverage)		0.335

(Gross internal area built as proportion of site area)

Site D

Location	Bishop's Stortford, East Hertfordshire
Type	Conventional. Real, existing site. Stand-alone scheme
Developer	Anonymous

Total size of site: (all the land the developer would have bought, including feeder and access roads but excluding major bypasses and distributor roads)	1.5 hectares (3.8 acres)
Standardised size of site: (as above but excluding public open space such as parks, greens, verges and recreation ground)	1.5 hectares (3.7 acres)
Developer's stated size of site: (where applicable)	1.5 hectares (3.7 acres)

Land use by size of footprint

Land use	As a percentage of total size
Public open space	3.4%
Peripheral and feeder roads	14.6%
Access roads and cul-de-sacs	9.9%
Public driveways, parking courtyards and shared space	0.0%
Private driveways	5.3%
Garages	4.0%
Private gardens	44.1%
Houses and flats	18.7%

Number of units

Type	All:	5+ beds	4 beds	3 beds	2 beds	1 bed
Detached	24	24	—	—	—	—
Semi-detached	—	—	—	—	—	—
Terraced	—	—	—	—	—	—
Apartments	—	—	—	—	—	—
TOTAL	24	24	—	—	—	—

Number of habitable rooms	216
Number of bed spaces	204
Area of all residential buildings (gross internal area)	6,340 m^2 (68,243 ft^2)

Densities	**On the basis of** Whole site area	Standardised site area
Dwellings (units) per hectare (acre)	16 (6)	16 (6)
Habitable rooms per hectare (acre)	140 (57)	144 (58)
Bed spaces per hectare (acre)	133 (54)	136 (55)
Plot ratio (coverage)		0.427

(Gross internal area built as proportion of site area)

Site E

Location	Chelmsford, Essex
Type	Exemplar. Real, existing site. Large phase on a larger scheme
Developer	Bryant Homes

Total size of site: (all the land the developer would have bought, including feeder and access roads but excluding major bypasses and distributor roads)	4.1 hectares (10.1 acres)
Standardised size of site: (as above but excluding public open space such as parks, greens, verges and recreation ground)	3.5 hectares (8.6 acres)
Developer's stated size of site: (where applicable)	3.5 hectares (8.7 acres)

Land use by size of footprint

Land use	As a percentage of total size
Public open space	13.3%
Peripheral and feeder roads, access roads and cul-de-sacs	19.5%
Public driveways, parking courtyards and shared space	2.2%
Private driveways, garages and private gardens	51.6%
Houses and flats	13.4%

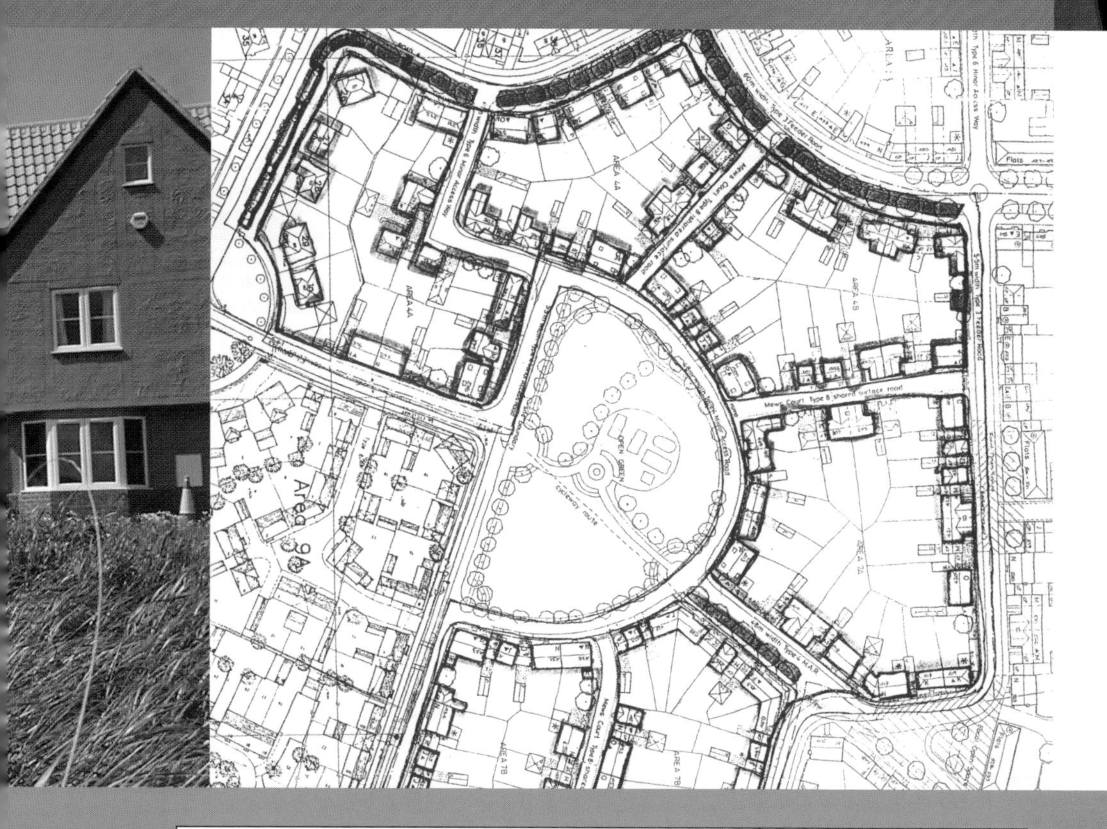

Number of units

Type	All:	5+ beds	4 beds	3 beds	2 beds	1 bed
Detached	—	—	—	—	—	—
Semi-detached	—	—	—	—	—	—
Terraced	—	—	—	—	—	—
Apartments	—	—	—	—	—	—
TOTAL	96	6	35	22	33	—

Number of habitable rooms	502
Number of bed spaces	500
Area of all residential buildings (gross internal area)	11,257 m^2 (121,166 ft^2)

Densities	**On the basis of**	
	Whole site area	Standardised site area
Dwellings (units) per hectare (acre)	23 (10)	28 (11)
Habitable rooms per hectare (acre)	123 (50)	144 (58)
Bed spaces per hectare (acre)	122 (50)	144 (58)
Plot ratio (coverage)		0.324

(Gross internal area built as proportion of site area)

Site F

Location	Chelmsford, Essex
Type	Conventional. Hypothetical site. Large phase on a larger scheme
Developer	N/A

Total size of site: (all the land the developer would have bought, including feeder and access roads but excluding major bypasses and distributor roads)	4.2 hectares (10.4 acres)
Standardised size of site: (as above but excluding public open space such as parks, greens, verges and recreation ground)	3.8 hectares (9.4 acres)
Developer's stated size of site: (where applicable)	N/A

Land use by size of footprint

Land use	As a percentage of total size
Public open space	11.0%
Peripheral and feeder roads, access roads and cul-de-sacs, public driveways, parking courtyards and shared space	17.5%
Private driveways, garages and private gardens	57%
Houses and flats	14.5%

Number of units

Type	All:	5+ beds	4 beds	3 beds	2 beds	1 bed
Detached	—	—	—	—	—	—
Semi-detached	—	—	—	—	—	—
Terraced	—	—	—	—	—	—
Apartments	—	—	—	—	—	—
TOTAL	101	23	27	51	—	—

Number of habitable rooms	616
Number of bed spaces	583
Area of all residential buildings (gross internal area)	11,326 m^2 (121,916 ft^2)

Densities

	On the basis of	
	Whole site area	Standardised site area
Dwellings (units) per hectare (acre)	24 (10)	27 (11)
Habitable rooms per hectare (acre)	146 (59)	162 (66)
Bed spaces per hectare (acre)	138 (56)	153 (62)
Plot ratio (coverage)		0.298

(Gross internal area built as proportion of site area)

Site G

Location	Aylesbury, Buckinghamshire
Type	Exemplar. Real, existing site. Small, late phase on a larger scheme
Developer	Bryant Homes

Total size of site: (all the land the developer would have bought, including feeder and access roads but excluding major bypasses and distributor roads)	1.8 hectares (4.6 acres)
Standardised size of site: (as above but excluding public open space such as parks, greens, verges and recreation ground)	1.8 hectares (4.4 acres)
Developer's stated size of site: (where applicable)	1.8 hectares (4.6 acres)

Land use by size of footprint

Land use	As a percentage of total size
Public open space	2.9%
Peripheral and feeder roads, access roads and cul-de-sacs	19.1%
Public driveways, parking courtyards and shared space	17.2%
Private driveways	4.9%
Garages	4.4%
Private gardens	32.8%
Houses and flats	18.7%

Number of units

Type	All:	5+ beds	4 beds	3 beds	2 beds	1 bed
Detached	—	—	—	—	—	—
Semi-detached	—	—	—	—	—	—
Terraced	—	—	—	—	—	—
Apartments	—	—	—	—	—	—
TOTAL	74	—	4	39	28	3

Number of habitable rooms	283
Number of bed spaces	279
Area of all residential buildings (gross internal area)	5,545 m^2 (59,690 ft^2)

Densities

	On the basis of Whole site area	Standardised site area
Dwellings (units) per hectare (acre)	40 (16)	42 (17)
Habitable rooms per hectare (acre)	152 (62)	159 (64)
Bed spaces per hectare (acre)	150 (61)	157 (63)
Plot ratio (coverage)		0.31

(Gross internal area built as proportion of site area)

Site H

Location	Aylesbury, Buckinghamshire
Type	Conventional. Hypothetical. Stand-alone scheme
Developer	N/A

Total size of site: (all the land the developer would have bought, including feeder and access roads but excluding major bypasses and distributor roads)	2.9 hectares (7.3 acres)
Standardised size of site: (as above but excluding public open space such as parks, greens, verges and recreation ground)	2.3 hectares (5.8 acres)
Developer's stated size of site: (where applicable)	3.0 hectares (7.4 acres)

Land use by size of footprint

Land use	As a percentage of total size
Public open space	25.3%
Peripheral and feeder roads,	14.7%
Access roads and cul-de-sacs	0.9%
Public driveways, parking courtyards and shared space	0.02%
Private driveways	6.6%
Garages	4.0%
Private gardens	35.78%
Houses and flats	12.7%

Number of units

Type	All:	5+ beds	4 beds	3 beds	2 beds	1 bed
Detached	39	—	31	8	—	—
Semi-detached	24	—	—	17	7	—
Terraced	13	—	—	—	13	—
Apartments	—	—	—	—	—	—
TOTAL	76	—	31	25	20	—

Number of habitable rooms	418
Number of bed spaces	409
Area of all residential buildings (gross internal area)	6,816 m^2 (73,364 ft^2)

Densities	**On the basis of**	
	Whole site area	Standardised site area
Dwellings (units) per hectare (acre)	26 (10)	32 (13)
Habitable rooms per hectare (acre)	141 (57)	178 (72)
Bed spaces per hectare (acre)	138 (56)	174 (71)
Plot ratio (coverage)		0.292

(Gross internal area built as proportion of site area)

Appendix 4.0

Step-by-step methodology

a4.0 Step-by-step methodology

1 Four locations in the south-east of England were selected.

2 An exemplar scheme in each area was then selected on the basis that each represented best practice and/or innovative design and layout and largely followed the urban design principles of PPG3.

3 A conventional housing scheme was then selected near to each of the exemplar schemes.

4 The build costs for both schemes in each area were measured. These costs excluded major remedial and infrastructure works and the costs of any section 106 agreements, including social housing (as these differ between sites). They did include landscaping costs and the costs of site roads, where they were provided by the developer. (A small flaw in this methodology is that it does not include the cost of site roads and layouts where they were provided by another developer. Ideally, they should be taken into account.)

5 Where costs were not available for the standard schemes, Davis Langdon & Everest constructed a hypothetical model of the scheme and its costs.

6 In each location, three local agents gave an open-market value for all the units on both of the schemes as at March 2002 *as if they were both built on the exemplar land*.

7 Where possible, actual values that were achieved on the schemes during March 2002 were obtained.

8 These real revenues were checked against the values given by the three local agents. If any valuer gave values which differed from the actual revenues by more than 20%, all the values given by that valuer were removed and not used. (In practice, this happened in just one case.)

9 The remaining values for each unit were averaged and then all unit average values were added together to give the total, gross development value (GDV).

10 The total build costs were subtracted from the total revenue to create a residual. (This residual represented the land value, central overheads and developer profit/margin — not just land value.)

11 The measurement of land was standardised on each site to:

— exclude major roads, bypasses, etc

— include all site roads, including minor peripheral roads

— measure roads on the periphery of the site which were shared with adjacent developments to the centre only

— exclude public open land regardless of whether the developer developed and landscaped it or not

— exclude land used for any section 106 agreements (such as land used for schools, community facilities and social housing, for example)

12 The residual value arrived at in 10 above was then divided by the number of hectares measured on the standardised basis derived in stage 11 above.

13 The resulting measure of the residual per hectare (or acre) then provided a measure of landowner/developer value that could be directly compared with other schemes in the same area and in other areas.

14 The exemplar schemes were compared with the conventional schemes in each location.

15 The differences between each scheme were analysed.

16 The possible impact of these differences on the residual value was examined.

Appendix 5.0

Illustrative example of the residual land calculation

a5.0 Illustrative example of the residual land calculation

		Site *X*	Site *Y*
A	Gross development value (GDV)	£70,000,000	£30,000,000
B	Land area (HSSM)	3.5	2
C	Total build costs	£25,000,000	£9,000,000
D	Residual value (A - C)	£45,000,000	£21,000,000
E	SDV per HSSM (D/B)	£12,857,000	£10,500,000
F	Percentage difference compared to other site	+ 22.4%	– 18.3%

Site *X* would appear to have a greater commercial value, developed in this way, than site *Y*.

The commercial value to the developer could be compared between sites in different locations by subtracting a standard land value figure for each location from the residual. The remaining figure would represent the profit and/or extra land buying power (which might enable the developer to secure the site against competition from other developers at the purchase stage) that is available to the developer.

Terms used:

GDV (gross development value)	Total of all average units values given by agents/valuers as if they were all built on the same site
Land area	Area of land using the standardised measure of site area (outlined in Appendix 4)
HSSM	Hectares of standardised site measurement
Total build costs	Total cost of developing the private housing units as defined in Appendix 2
Residual value	Sum available to the developer to cover land costs, central overheads and profit
Standardised development value (SDV)	Residual value as defined above

Acknowledgements

Acknowledgements

Thanks are due to Davis Langdon & Everest for their contribution to the cost analysis in this study. Also, to Professor Alan Hooper at Cardiff University for the Literature Review and the helpful comments and encouragement he gave at the outset of the study.

This research would not have been possible without the help and cooperation of the developers of both the exemplar and conventional schemes in the case studies. Our particular thanks are due to Bryant Homes, Countryside Homes, Fairview, St James Homes and another developer, who prefers to remain anonymous, for their time, effort and input into this study.

Thanks are also due to the valuers at various offices of estate agents: Bradford and Bingley, Brown and Merry, FPDSavills, Nicholas Pallet, Peter Anstee & Co and Your Move.

Finally, the authors would like to thank CABE for their considerable time and effort in steering this project over the past year or so and to thank them, ODPM, Design for Homes and the House Builders Federation for sponsoring the study.

Steering Group

David Birkbeck	Design for Homes
John Miles	Ove Arup Partnership
John Weir	Haute Future
Christina Golton	ODPM
Stephen Mullin	ODPM
Simon Pinnegar	ODPM
Kate Anderton	CABE
Ben Castell	CABE
Jon Rouse	CABE

Photography credits

Photographs on front cover and pages 7, 11, 15, 25, 35, 45, 49, 53, 65, 83, 85 and 87 courtesy of Mark Ellis

Photograph of Site A, page 66, courtesy of PRP + Daniel Thistlethwaite